The Essential Chuang Tzu

The Essential
CHUANG TZU

Translated from the Chinese by

SAM HAMILL and J. P. SEATON

SHAMBHALA
Boston & London
1999

SHAMBHALA PUBLICATIONS, INC.
Horticultural Hall
300 Massachusetts Avenue
Boston, Massachusetts 02115
www.shambhala.com

9 8 7 6 5 4 3

Printed in the United States of America

♾ This edition is printed on acid-free paper that meets
the American National Standards Institute z39.48 Standard.
Distributed in the United States by Random House, Inc.,
and in Canada by Random House of Canada Ltd

*The Library of Congress catalogs the hardcover edition of
this book as follows:*
Chuang-tzu.
[Nan-hua ching English]
The essential teachings of Chuang-Tzu/translated by
Sam Hamill and J. P. Seaton.
p.   cm.
ISBN 1-57062-336-8 (alk.paper)
ISBN 1-57062-457-7 (pbk.)
I. Hamill, Sam. II. Seaton, Jerome P. III. Title.
BL1900.C46E5   1998   97-38797
299.51482—dc21   CIP

TO *Burton Watson*

AND TO
*Christopher Yohmei Blasdel,
Jerry Douglas, Russ Barenberg,
and Edgar Meyer*

Contents

Foreword

IF ALL THE CHINESE POETS, PAINTERS, AND WRITERS WHO ever lived were queried and asked to name just one book of their favorite reading, the nomination would certainly go to the writings of Master Chuang. The book that came to be known as the *Chuang Tzu* is an anthology of early Taoist thought. At least seven of its thirty-three surviving chapters can be attributed to the philosopher Chuang Chou (369–286 BCE). The book's appeal to Chinese intellectuals through the millennia derives as much from its content as from its style. Chuang Tzu's message of freedom and nonconformity liberates the Chinese mind and provides a wholesome antidote to the ethical and social values embraced by the Confucianists. The writer was a born storyteller and a supreme artist with words: he used all the resources of language that were at his disposal—from *anaphora* to *zeugma*, hyperboles and litotes, parallelism and antithesis, paradox and humor, and, most devastating of all, a device known as the non sequitur. Chuang Tzu drew from a vast storehouse of ancient Chinese myths, legends, and unrecorded history, as well as from an encyclopedic knowledge of what may be regarded as the "unnatural natural history," to weave together—by means of parables and anecdotal debates—the vision of a skeptic and mystic, in a world beset by constant and dangerous moral choices.

Complete or partial English translations of *Chuang Tzu* are available in many versions—including those from the last century by Herbert Giles (1889) and James Legge (1891); the more scholarly, modern contributions by Arthur Waley (1939) and Burton Watson (1964 and 1968); the more poetically nuanced ones by Lin Yutang (1948) and Thomas Merton (1965); and the still more recent scholarship of Angus C. Graham (1981) and Victor H. Mair (1994). However, Sam Hamill and Sandy Seaton's new retranslation of this much-beloved Taoist classic has much to commend itself, largely by virtue of its boldness of approach and its innovative use of language. Let me elaborate.

The book is a collaborative effort by two of the most talented wordsmiths of their generation, and it employs a language that is vibrant and colorful. It aims at readability even to the extent of ignoring formal fidelity in translation. In tackling the problem of translating from one language to another, it has been generally assumed that there are two approaches possible: the literal or the free. But the more seasoned translators have come to realize that there is a third alternative, which is preferable. And that is to temper faithfulness to the original with expressiveness in the target language and to combine straightforwardness with elegance; ultimately, to achieve what have been recognized as the three desiderata of translation: *hsin* (fidelity), *ta* (expressiveness), and *ya* (elegance).

For a translation from a tersely worded philosophical text, it must be obvious to many that a literal approach is the least rewarding and ought not to be exclusively relied upon. If care is not taken in this regard, one can expect to find, as one does in Fung Yu-lan's translation, such a passage: "The universe is a finger; all things are a horse. The possible is possible. The impossible is impossible. The *Tao* makes things and they are what they are. What are they? They are what they are. What are they not? They are not what they are not" (*Chuang-tzu*, 1931; 1989 reprint p. 45). Even in the newest, more lucid translation by Victor Mair (*Wandering on the Way*, 1994), one encounters this passage as: "Heaven and earth are the same as a finger; the myriad things are the same as a horse. Affirmation lies in our affirming; denial lies in our denying. A way comes into being through our walking upon it; a thing is so because people say that it is. Why are things so? They are so because we declare them to be so. Why are things not so? They are not so because we declare them to be not so" (p. 16). Contrast the above with the bold reduction of these arguments into just a few words by Hamill and Seaton: "Heaven-and-earth is one finger. All ten thousand things are one horse. Okay? Not okay. Okay? Okay. Walk in the Tao. Accomplish it all. Say words, and they're so. How so? Is so? How not so? Not so *so*!" (chapter two). Deliberate mischief? Absolutely justifiable.

Chuang Tzu, one must also bear in mind, is not only a philosopher but a poet. In one passage, Chuang Tzu used the noun *spring* as a verb, which so captivated Burton Watson that, as he explained in the Introduction (*The Complete Works of Chuang Tzu*, p. 19), he attempted to emulate it by translating the passage as: " . . . never be at a loss with joy . . . and *make it be spring* with everything" [italics mine] (chapter five, *Ibid.*, p. 74). How much more natural to find the same passage in Hamill and Seaton translated as: "Never let joy be lost . . . eternally in the springtime of things," though one knows that it is not a literal translation.

Throughout the translation, the two translators dare to be original (and controversial), occasionally inventing a new idiom, as seen in their onomatopoeic use of words such as *hua* or *kerplop*—almost intentionally to suggest some of the wit and whimsicality of the original text. Now the characters who appeared in the stories and anecdotes in the *Chuang Tzu* can, broadly speaking, be classified into three categories: the first consisting of historical figures like Confucius or the logician Hui Tzu (Hui Shih, circa 370–310? BCE), the second consisting of mythological or legendary beings like Fu Hsi (China's Prometheus) or the Yellow Emperor. But a third and equally large group is made up of figures,

or creatures, created from the baseless fabric of the author's vision—like a Pistol or a Caliban—to whom Chuang Tzu often gave
fanciful names. And these proper names, if allowed to remain in
their original, transliterated status, will mean very little to English readers. But if an attempt is made by the translator to allude
to the moral or physical qualities of this person (or creature) so
described or caricatured, it poses a challenge of the greatest mag-
nitude. One character is given by Watson in the Chinese original
as "Nieh Ch'ueh," but the same figure appears in A. C. Graham's
translation as "Gaptooth" and in Victor Mair's as "Gnaw Gap."
Hamill and Seaton gave this name as "Mr. Chipped Tooth."

Improvements of this sort abound in the various chapters of
this new version. Another example is found in chapter eleven,
where a character with the name of Cloud General (Yun-chiang)
is said to roam the universe in search of an answer for good government and chances to meet a being who lectures him on the
value of transcendence through nonaction. This character in the
Chuang Tzu is given the name of Hung-meng with the second
character, *meng*, written without the water-radical. Whether or
not the change was deliberate on Chuang Tzu's part, one can
never be sure today without access to more reliable textual evidence. But most commentators, from Hsiang Hsiu (d. 272) and
Kuo Hsiang (d. 312) down to our time, have accepted this rhymed-
compound or binome as a cognate of *meng-hung* with the second
character written with the water-radical. While the compound of
Hung-meng occurs only in *Chuang Tzu*, the compound in the reverse order of *meng-hung* (with the water radical) occurs three
times in the *Hua-nan Tzu* (circa 140 BCE), another ancient Taoist
classic, and it is always glossed by early commentators as meaning "the undifferentiated ether of the universe before creation."
But, when written *without* the water-radical, the word *meng* by
itself means "ignorance"; the word occurs in the *Book of
Changes (I-ching)* as number four of the sixty-four hexagrams,
translated by Richard Wilhelm as "Youthful Folly"—it is made
up of the trigrams *ken*, above, meaning "keeping still, mountain," and *k'an*, below, meaning "the abysmal, water" (I, 20).

And, since the Chinese language allows a word to have many meanings, it would not be wrong to accept the first word *hung* as also meaning "a large wild goose" (and that meaning also goes back to ancient times, to the *Book of Poetry*, or *Shih-ching*).

With all these options open, how would a translator approach the task of translating the name of this singular creature? And the manner by which he is introduced? Here is Herbert Giles: "The Spirit of the Clouds . . . happened to fall in with the Vital Principle. The latter was slapping his ribs and hopping about" (p. 129). "Vital Principle" was introduced as "Vast Obscurity" in Victor Mair (p. 97), where he was said to be "just at that moment enjoying himself by slapping his thighs and hopping like a sparrow." And this creature addressing the Cloud Chief was described by Watson as "Big Concealment, still thigh-slapping and sparrow-hopping" (p. 121). All these are worthy attempts at rendering this highly amusing episode in modern-day English. But the first prize, I dare say, must go to Hamill and Seaton, whose version reads: "Cloud General . . . bumped into Big Goose Dummy. Drumming on his tummy, Big Goose Dummy was about to take off like a hopping sparrow." Punning, of course, involves the risk of censure by the purist, especially when an attempt at etymological reconstruction may turn out to be wrong or misguided. But a success of this sort also needs to be recognized: at the very least it evokes the most glorious as well as the most glaring of the kinds of excesses indulged in by Ezra Pound.

Thus, a much-admired Taoist classic of ancient China—which age cannot wither nor whose infinite wisdom, grace, and subtlety can be staled by numberless borrowings and pilferage through the ages—has been given a new lease on life, in colloquial American English that is exciting to read.

IRVING YUCHENG LO
Fearrington Village
Palm Sunday, 1998

Translators' Introduction

No one wrote the classic book named for the grandfather of philosophical Taoism, Chuang Tzu. Neither Master Chuang Chou nor the other ancient Chinese philosophers of the Chou dynasty (third century BCE) wrote books. They recorded verses, songs, brief essays, conversations, and anecdotes, writing them on strips of bamboo that eventually were bound together and rolled into scrolls. Each "chapter" of *Chuang Tzu* was composed of one scroll. It is generally thought that chapters 1 through 7, the "Inner Chapters," are the compilation of Chuang Tzu himself or of his immediate followers, and that the "outer" and "miscellaneous" chapters were added, edited, or abridged by various hands. At the time of the Han dynasty (first century BCE), the Imperial Library edition contained fifty-two chapters. The present form of the "complete" *Chuang Tzu* in thirty-three chapters was edited by Kuo Hsiang in the third century CE.

Chuang Tzu inhabits a territory where history and myth become one. Little is certain about his origins or his life. Like the Ch'an (Zen) Buddhist masters who, several centuries later, drew heavily from both his technique and his teaching, Chuang Tzu believed that we are each the source of our own suffering and that much of our suffering is a direct result of our insistence on judging things "good" or "bad" while refusing to accept what simply *is*. He believed that people waste their lives clinging to *things*. His use of paradox and startling juxtaposition probably inspired the Zen koan. Chuang Tzu delighted in questions that demolish our ridiculous insistence on "rational" behavior.

The teachings of Master Chuang, along with those of the equally mythologized Lao Tzu and his *Tao Te Ching* (if there *was* a Lao Tzu and if he *did* write *Tao Te Ching*), are the primary teachings of philosophical Taoism. Chuang Tzu lived in a time when the literate classes were schooled in the moralistic teachings of Confucius, especially the *Classic of Filial Piety* and the *Analects*, so it is hardly surprising when the Taoist sage skewers the pompous and scoffs at conventional assumptions about "righteousness" and "benevolence." He was as devoted to what Carl Jung, more than two millennia later, called "self-actualization" or "individuation" as was Confucius to the ideal of social benevolence. In the centuries that followed, Taoism provided a balance to Confucianism, and the two teachings were blended in social philosophy. Buddhism eventually provided the third of the interlocking Three Systems (*san chiao*) that dominated Chinese thinking and social policy into the present century.

The importance of Chuang Tzu is almost inestimable. He has been studied by every major Chinese, Japanese, Korean, and Southeast Asian poet and philosopher of the past two thousand years. Li Po quotes him; Tu Fu turns to him for solace; Bashō won't leave home without him. In the West, Ezra Pound, ever the Confucian, quarrels with him; Gary Snyder becomes his companion. He is read for pleasure, for edification, and for sheer, unfettered delight.

Given Chuang Tzu's convictions about language—specifically, that words have no absolute meanings except as can be mutually agreed on—and given his insistence on centering and spontaneity as the source of art and life, the book called *Chuang Tzu* must be approached by the translator as a work of art presenting an enormous range of problems and possibilities. We have tried to develop a systematic approach to our translation in an effort to record and mirror Chuang Tzu's art, while trying hard not to try *too* hard.

We have been as consistent as possible in the rendering of terms from one chapter to the next in order to reduce confusion, even though we know that little or none of the material following the "Inner Chapters" was composed by Chuang Tzu himself. His followers and companions knew him better than we can. When they use his vocabulary, it is usually with a clear and conspicuous purpose in mind. Thus we are convinced that where the English language context may call for variety in the rendering of a given term, consistency in translating such terms almost always provides a greater depth, as well as a broader texture, allowing the *recreation* (in both senses of that word) of conscious irony.

T'ien hsia, for instance, literally means "beneath heaven" and refers to "the empire," the legal realm of the legitimate emperor or "Son of Heaven." It is a consciously political term. But to Chuang Tzu it also meant "the whole world," or "all that is under the sky," or even "the totality of phenomenal reality on earth." And in some contexts it is used to mean simply "everybody." Other translators have used *the state, the world,* and so forth, depending on context. We've kept the set phrase *All-under-heaven* because we believe that, as in the original, its repetition in various contexts allows the ironic play between meanings such as "the empire" and plain old "everybody" to resonate, clarify, or magnify.

Translating the terms *t'ien, ti,* and *jen* (heaven, earth, and people) presents another set of problems. *T'ien*, "heaven," does not mean, as it might in folk religion, a place with angels and pearly gates and a white-bearded old granddaddy, and it doesn't suggest a god such as Yahweh. Nor can it be translated merely as *laws of nature*, or *natural law*, although that is part of its meaning. It may mean "sky," or something like "nature," or something like "god." We have chosen to translate it literally as *heaven*, to allow for an accretion of meaning depending on context.

Jen, a simple two-stroke stick figure, is the Chinese character for "person" or "humankind." Only in specific contexts does it mean "male." It is also used in certain contexts to refer to all things artificial, that is, made by human hands.

The three-word set *t'ien*, *ti*, and *jen* was, for Chuang Tzu, the denotation of a philosophical or even cosmological concept. Heaven is all yang, earth all yin, and humankind composed of a balance of the two. Together they were known as the Three Powers, forces thought to rule human life and society and thus were considered in decision making at every level.

This translation makes use of more etymological study than probably any previous version. Particularly in its early periods, when written vocabulary was limited and pictographic and ideographic elements still outnumbered the less interesting, partly phonetic elements (that are 80 percent of modern characters), it is sometimes easier to see the range of meaning of a Chinese character by analyzing its meaningful elements than by consulting a dictionary. For example, look up the characters *hao* and *jen* (a homonym of the aforementioned *jen*) and you will find "good" as the definition of each. *Hao* is a drawing of a woman with an infant, a perfectly eloquent and earthy word. *Jen*, on the other hand, is an abbreviated human figure beside the number two, a wonderful *abstraction* meant to represent the way humans will or must treat one another because they are human—species solidarity, a great idea first promoted to the level of philosophy by Confucius himself.

Master Chuang, like the great T'ang poets who went to school on his work, clearly made artistic use of visual elements in written characters. Thus we have been required to pay attention to the semiological as well as the etymological aspects of his language. An author may create strong visual reinforcement for purely linguistic effects by choosing characters with pictorial elements that suit the theme, even when the meanings of the characters are not dependent on the particular pictorial element in

xviii

question. To represent "fecund moisture," for instance, one may choose characters—nouns, adjectives, verbs, and even pronouns and prepositions—that contain any of several representations of water: the full character for water, reduced in size and placed within, above, or beneath the main body of the "new" character; or three little dots, droplets of water, placed to the left; or even a broken line over a full line over a broken line, a graph that forms one of the eight trigrams of the *I Ching*.

The famous poem "Quiet Night," by the T'ang poet Li Po, uses only twenty written characters. But the poet includes two moon characters and four other moons: two in the repeated word *bright*, one in the preposition *before* (or *in front of*), and one hidden in the verb *to gaze*. Fully 30 percent of the words in the poem contain visual representations of the moon, an object and an image that is central to the theme of the poem. "Quiet Night" is a renowned tour de force, but the technique is not unusual. All the punning on feet that takes place in chapter 5 of *Chuang Tzu* is drawn directly from the original, where the foot element is conspicuously present in a much higher proportion of characters than in any other chapter. (Feet, particularly amputated feet, remain a source of cautionary and faintly macabre humor throughout the book.) Where Master Chuang's language offers such resources, we, as translators, have received them gratefully.

A dizzying array of literary techniques is brought to bear in the written composition of *Chuang Tzu*, particularly in the "Inner Chapters." It remains nevertheless a compilation of verses, fables, recorded conversations, and anecdotes in the classic oral tradition, tales meant as much to be listened to as studied textually. With this in mind, we have sought a prose style that will fall as naturally on the ear as good conversation, without sacrificing the elliptical or enigmatic qualities of the original. Master Chuang enjoyed rambling, so much so that he felt no need to bind this thought to that, this tale to that verse. Connections are there more often than not, but they are there to be discovered by the engaged reader. The great Taoist did not love thoughts and did not cling to them; yet the rhythms and marvels of the thinking mind engaged in the process of spontaneous self-revelation are an almost constant presence in *Chuang Tzu*. His mind and writing are the mind and writing of a poet, whether in prose or in verse.

Our translation is based on the text available in the Harvard-Yenching Concordance. The concordance itself was particularly useful in enabling us to check the frequency of use of certain pieces of vocabulary and even, with a little manipulation, the frequency of use of phonetic and signific elements that might have semiological significance. Without this great segment of the wonderful Harvard-Yenching Index Series, we would have had little to support our intuitions. We also made constant reference to Weiger and Karlgren, the *Shuo-wen*, and the Harvard-Yenching *Erh Ya*, for etymologies; and Chinese and Japanese commentaries, particularly to Wang Shu-min's remarkably succinct assemblage of text and commentaries, *Chuang Tzu ch'iao ch'uan* (Taipei, 1988).

We also turned once again, with genuine pleasure, to the available English translations, including the free poetic partial translations of Thomas Merton and Martin Buber, the latter translated from the German by Jonathan Herman in *I and Tao* (State University Press of New York, Albany, 1996). Any translator of this ancient text stands on the shoulders of, if not always giants, an at least slightly leaning tower of predecessors that includes both Chinese scholars and modern translators. Some have one leg shorter than the other, perhaps having lost a foot (or a footing) somewhere along the way. The text has been amazingly well maintained, and often brilliantly interpreted in both commentaries and translations, which have aided us every step of the way.

The Essential Chuang Tzu

Free and Easy Wandering

[CHAPTER 1]

Deep in the Northern Darkness there is a fish called K'un, so large its breadth cannot be measured. But suddenly—hua!—it metamorphoses into a bird called a P'eng* with a back so long there's no way to know where it ends. Only with enormous effort can it rise on huge wings that cover the sky like clouds across the heavens. What a *bird*! When it is moved to fly, it soars all the way to the Southern Darkness, which is also called the Pool of Heaven.

That honorable tome *Best Laughs of Ch'i* records many wonders, including this: "When the P'eng takes off for the Southern Darkness, the ocean's waves are beaten flat across a thousand miles or more. Its great wings flap and it rises to thirty thousand miles in the sky, then flies south for three months before landing. Wild horses stampeding? Dirt and dust fly up. Every living thing is thrown into chaos by the P'eng's turbulent descent."

*See glossary.

That bluest blue of the heavens—is that a real color or just the result of it being so very far away? When the P'eng looks down, all it sees is blue. We all know shallow water will not lift and hold a boat. A little water poured into a crack in the floor is enough to float a mustard seed, but place the cup in the water poured from it into that crack, and shallow water leaves it grounded. Likewise with the wind: when it's not strong, it can't help lift big wings. It takes a gale force wind of ninety thousand *li* for a P'eng to ride the wind, sky across its back, and nothing to hinder its southward journey.

The cicada and the fledgling dove both laugh, saying, "When we want to fly, we can easily reach the lower branches of small trees; or, if we fall short, we return to the ground. Why would *anyone* want to fly up thirty thousand miles and head south?"

For a hike in the woods near home, one usually takes along three meals and returns well fed. Traveling thirty miles, one grinds grain the night before departure; those who travel a thousand miles require three months' provisions. But a couple of weevils in the meal won't know the difference.

Small understanding doesn't get to where great understanding gets. Youth doesn't know what age teaches. How do I know? The morning mushroom doesn't know dawn from dusk. The summer cicada knows neither spring nor autumn. And so it is with youth.

In Southern Ch'u, there is a tree called the Dark Spirit Tree. A full five hundred years is only a single spring to this tree, five hundred years merely a single autumn. In really ancient times, there was the Tachun tree that counted eight thousand years as one spring, another eight thousand for a single autumn. And yet Master P'eng, who lived a mere nineteen hundred years, is all one hears about these days. Everyone's just *got* to be like him! How pathetic!

In *T'ang's Interrogations of Ch'i*, the story is repeated: "In the bare bald north, there is a dark sea called the Pool of Heaven, in which there is a fish called K'un that is thousands of miles across and no-one-knows how long. And there is a bird called P'eng, with a back like Mount T'ai and wings as broad as the clouds in the heavens. It flaps up hurricanes as it climbs thousands of miles, cutting through the very souls of clouds, lifting the blue sky. Then it turns south without resting until it arrives in the depths of the Southern Dark Sea."

The sparrow, less than a foot in length, laughs, saying, "Oh, *that* one! What does he think he's doing? A little hop and a flap and I'm up; a few yards and I'm down again. I flutter among weeds and brambles. Now *that's* flying to get where you're going! And that one! Just where does he think *he's* going?" There's that distinction between Great and Small!

And it is equally true of the one who knows how to perform efficiently at a certain official position, one whose behavior may serve as a model for neighbors, one whose powers may serve the needs of a certain lord, or even of a state. Such a person makes a self-assessment in the same way small creatures do. Master Sung Jung Tzu would burst out laughing. The whole world could prize him and he would work no harder; the whole world could call him wrong, and yet he would persist. He knows what is Inner and what is Outer; he knows the difference between true honor and disgrace. It's as simple as that. In this world, few can equal him when it comes to instinctively knowing and doing what is right. But despite his proximity to perfection, he has not yet attained the perfection of a tree.

Lieh Tzu made the wind his chariot and traveled lightly and with considerable ease. How wonderful to travel fifteen full days before needing to return! Few in this world ever find a comparable happiness. And yet, despite successfully avoiding walking, he was nonetheless dependent. Had he mounted the Rightness-of-Heaven-and-Earth and driven the changes of the six energies [*ch'i*], *then* he could wander endlessly. What then would he be dependent upon? So it is said, "The one who's made it *there* has no self; the spiritual leader does no deed; the true sage has no name."

Yao tried to pass the rulership of All-under-heaven to Hsu Yu, saying, "The sun and moon are out, and yet the torches remain burning. Doesn't too much light just make things all the more difficult? If we irrigate during the rainy season, aren't we exercising poor management? If you would only stand and assume your rightful place, All-under-heaven would be well governed. Although I try to model my conduct on yours, I can be no more than the 'personator' at the sacrifices whose duty it is to represent the spirits of departed ancestors. I see what a mess I've made of things! Please accept rulership."

Hsu Yu replied, "You're ruling All-under-heaven, so it's being ruled. If I assumed power, what would I be taking but a title? Aren't titles and names merely the servants, the familiar guests of the real? And why would I want to become a servant of myself? The little sparrow nesting in the forest needs only a single branch; the mole drinking from the river drinks but one bellyful. Go home, my lord, and sit under a shady tree. I have no use at all for All-under-heaven. When the cook fails to govern his kitchen, the high priest and the 'personator' don't leap over wine casks in a rush to succeed him."

Chieh Wu said to Lien Shu, "I listened to the Madman of Ch'u, Chieh Yu. Big talk. But there was no thusness in it. It went out and on and on, but it never came back to anything. I was shocked and frightened by it. He went on and on like the River of Heaven, flowing without end. It was just too much. And all without the warmth of human feeling."

Lien Shu asked, "What did he say?"

"He said, 'On far off Ku She Mountain, there is a feminine spirit with flesh and bone like ice and snow, gentle and sweet as a virgin. She doesn't eat the Five Grains, but sips the breeze and the dew. She climbs the highest clouds and drives a chariot drawn by flying dragons, wandering the Four Seas at her leisure. Her

4

spirit, when concentrated, keeps things from decaying and brings crops to fruition.' I thought him obviously mad, so gave his words no credence."

Lien Shu replied thoughtfully, "So. So it is indeed. The blind cannot know the beauty of emblem or artifice; the deaf cannot perceive the awesome sound of bell and drum. But how is it possible that deafness and blindness inhabit only flesh and bone? There is deafness and blindness in the comprehending mind as well. So it is with Chieh Yu's words. And yet there *is* this feminine spirit, this feminine principle that can bring the ten thousand things into One. Our world, however, remains attached to disorder, everyone willing to accept All-under-heaven as their charge today. But this spirit lies beyond worldly harm. If waters should rise and flood the sky, she wouldn't drown; if the Great Drought returned, if mountains and hillsides ran with molten stone and iron, she wouldn't burn. You could smelt and cast sage emperors like Yao and Shun from the scraps and dust she leaves behind. Why would she wish to stoop to be in the service of mere things?"

THERE ONCE WAS A HAT-SELLER FROM SUNG WHO BROUGHT a load of ceremonial caps to Yueh, unaware that Yueh folk shave and tattoo their heads and so have no use for hats. Yao ruled benevolently, governing a peace that reached the Four Seas, but after venturing out to see off the Four Sages of Ku She Mountain on the sunlit side of the Fen River, he forgot all about All-under-heaven and sat in a wall-eyed daze.

HUI TZU SAID TO CHUANG TZU, "THE KING OF WEI SENT me the seeds of a giant gourd. When I planted them, they grew to the size of five bushels. But if you fill one with soup or water, it's much too heavy to lift; if you cut one to make a ladle, it's too flat and straight, making it awkward to use. They were huge! But useless. So I smashed them."

Chuang Tzu replied, "You, sir, are very clumsy when it comes to the uses of the great. In Sung, there were some folks who created a wonderful salve for chapped hands. Whole generations of silk bleachers used it faithfully. Then one day a stranger heard about the salve and offered them a hundred pieces of gold to reveal the secret. When the clan gathered to discuss the offer, one man said, 'We've made this salve for generations and have nothing to show for it but a few pieces of gold. Now, in one morning, we can make a hundred. I say sell it.' The stranger bought the secret recipe. And off he went for an audience with the King of Wu. There was trouble with Yueh—as always—and he got himself appointed general. That winter, they fought a great naval battle, utterly routing the Yueh people, and the salve helped the Wu navy crews. He was rewarded with a fiefdom drawn from Yueh territory. So. In their ability to treat chapped hands, the stranger and the clan were equal. But one ended up with a fiefdom while others couldn't escape the bleach and labors of the silk trade. It's only a difference in *use*.

"Now you have five-bushel gourds. Why didn't you make a tub of one, or a boat to float on lakes and rivers? You complain that they were too awkward to use to hold anything, when in fact they already contained *nothing*. Your head's still stuck in the brambles!"

Hui Tzu sniffed and replied, "I know a huge tree local folks call the *trea*, trunk so thick, so gnarled and knotty that the carpenter can't cut it for use, branches too twisted for compass or square. Although it stands beside a busy road, no carpenter ever gives it a second look. Your words are just as big, just as knotty and as worthless! Nobody has any use for *them*, either!"

Chuang Tzu laughed. "Haven't you ever watched a wildcat or a weasel as it keeps low to the ground, bowing in wait for its prey before it leaps east or west, never avoiding high or low, only to end up snared in some hunter's net? But look at the yak: big as clouds in the sky, big enough to call *huge*, but useless when it comes to catching mice.

"Now you have this huge tree. You think it's terrible that no one can cut it for use. Why not let it be a tree?—in the Village of No-Thing, where the wilds spread out in every direction toward No-Place. Sit beneath it and master the art of nondoing. Wander freely, easily into dreams beneath it. Forget the ax—nothing can harm it. Nothing can possibly be of use. Where's the problem?"

All Things Being Equal

[CHAPTER 2]

Nan-kuo Tzu-ch'i leaned on his armrest while sitting in meditation. He looked out toward the heavens. His breath came softly, steadily. He appeared to have lost himself. His attendant, Yen-ch'eng Tzu-yu, standing beside him, asked, "What sort of concentration is this? Can you really turn your body into a withered tree? Your heart into cold ashes? The man who leans here is not the one who did before."

Tzu-ch'i replied, "Dear Yen, it is good of you to ask. Just now, I lost myself. Could you tell? You've heard the piping of people, but not yet of the piping of earth; when you know the piping of earth, you will not yet have heard the piping of the heavens."

"I dare ask their secrets," Tzu-yu stated.

Tzu-ch'i smiled. "Well. Hmm. When the Great Clod belches, a prompt response may squelch it. But once begun, ten thousand holes emit an angry wail. Are you the only one who hasn't heard the roaring? In the high mountain forests there are huge trees—a hundred feet around—ringed with cavities, holes like noses, mouths, ears, like sockets or goblets, like mortars. Like babies, they begin with grunts and 'wah-wahs' and such. And then there are roars like the surf's, sounds like shouted orders, raging screams, growls and snarls. When a breeze comes up they call, 'Hooo,' and as the breezes pass they cry, 'Yooo.' Small cold breezes make small harmonies; whirlwinds make great harmonies. And when the great winds pass, all the cavities and holes are filled with emptiness again. Have you alone not heard it, not seen things wavering, quivering, only to return to rest again?"

Tzu-yu said, "So the piping of the earth comes from its many holes, just as the pipes and flutes we play come from varieties of bamboo. But may I be so bold as to inquire about the piping of the heavens?"

Tzu-ch'i said, "It blows upon the ten thousand things, yet blows upon no two the same. It permits each to become itself, each choosing to be itself. But from whom, such a breath?"

GREAT UNDERSTANDING CUTS ITSELF OFF ANDS FALLS IDLE; small understanding grows lazier still. Big words can burst into flames and begin conflagrations; small words are mere chatter. The souls of sleepers may wander off in search of mates, but when awakened they ally themselves with all that is outer, their hearts wrestling with indecision, deceit, and seductions. Small fears unsettle the heart; great fears twist the bowels with indecision.

Some souls fly off like arrows from the crossbow, turning every this and that into a "right" or a "wrong." Some remain stuck like squatters guarding whatever it is they think they've won. They die like autumn into winter, dwindling like daylight in the late season. They drown in their own maneuverings. No one can help them rise and begin anew. Their own choices determine their oppression. They grow old and their blood grows thin and death draws near, yet none can look deeply enough into the heart to find the sun's yang, and rise with it to begin again.

9

Anger and delight; happiness and grief; anxiety and regret; fickleness and stubbornness; modesty and willfulness; insolence and toadying—music out of emptiness. Fungus sprouts in mustiness. Day and night follow each other. Who knows which came first or what are the sources of the sun and moon?

Enough. Aren't they enough, sunrise and sunset? Are they not our progenitors? Without them, there is no I. Without "I," there is no thing to cling. Although this knowledge is clear to me, I do not know what's responsible for making it so. It's as if there were such a thing as a True Lord, but I find no evidence of such—I can go forward believing, and yet I can find no such form. Is there fact without form? The hundred joints, the nine openings, the six viscera come from the womb and I, a child, exist. Which of these parts shall I then treat as one of my family? Will you speak up for all of them? You *will* have a favorite. If they are all your servants and handmaids, consider: are servants and maids sufficient to rule as governors? Can they all take turns at governance? Is there a True Lord among them? If I should seek to ascertain the facts of this and cannot, the facts remain unaffected.

From the moment we first accomplish a form for ourselves, we cannot forget that we merely await its exhaustion. We raise our swords to fence with the things of this world or we waste them, as they waste us, like a horse raced into utter exhaustion. No one can stop us. Isn't it pathetic? Heartless? Winter comes, the string of our lives runs out, and we have slaved to accomplish an end we never see, hearts wasted in wearisome labors, never knowing a home we may return to. Isn't it pitiful? You may say, "At least I'm not dead," but what good is that? Your form will change, and your heart with it. Can't we call this truly pitiful? But this is human life. Can it be lost among small weeds? Is it only I, myself, who am lost? Are others not equally lost?

If you follow the dictates of an accomplished heart, you have found a teacher. And who can fail to find such a teacher? Must it be that only those who understand the cycles of succession choose the heart as their teacher? Fools, too, may do so. But to choose a right or wrong without an accomplished heart is like departing now for Yueh, only to arrive there long ago. This is confusing what does not exist with what does, trying to make something from nothing. Even the great Sage Yu couldn't find a way to do that! How could I alone learn how this might be done?

But words, words are *not* mere puffs of breath. Words speak. But if definitions have not already been agreed upon, can they really say anything? What differentiates words from the chirps of fledgling birds, if anything? Is there a difference?

If the Tao remained obscured, how could we know the natural from the artificial? And if words are clouded, where is the "right" or the "wrong"? Tao! How could we go on without it? How can words exist and still be impossible? Tao is obscured by small "accomplishments" in the same way words are obscured by rhetorical flourishes.

Thus we arrive at the rights and wrongs of the Confucians and the Mohists: one takes the other's right as wrong and its wrong for right. If you want to right wrongs and wrong rights, nothing serves like the bright light of this sort of wisdom. There is no thing that is not that; there is no thing that is not this. That doesn't see itself as that. Self-knowledge precedes knowing others. So it's said, "*That* arises out of *this*, but *this* is also caused by exactly *that*. This is the theory that *this* and *that* are born together." And although this is true enough, where there's birth, there's death; where there's death, birth. Where there's a possible, there is the impossible; with the impossible, the possible. Cause right and you cause wrong; cause wrong, cause right. Right? So be it.

The sage doesn't belabor the point but stands revealed in clear daylight. He knows all this: that this is that and that is this, and he knows also that the *that* and the *this* make One of right and wrong. Does he still *have* a this and a that, or does he not have a this or that?

When even This and That have lost all sense of themselves, we call it the Pivot of the Tao, and when the pivot is born into the middle of the great circle, it serves without end. What is so is eternally so; what is not is not forever. And they say, "There is nothing like the light of wisdom."

11

To use a finger to make the point that a finger is not a finger is not as good as using a nonfinger to make the same point. To use a horse to prove that a horse is not a horse is not as good as to use a nonhorse to prove that a horse is not a horse. Heaven-and-earth is one finger. All ten thousand things are one horse. Okay? Not okay. Okay? Okay.

Walk in the Tao. Accomplish it all. Say words, and they're *so*. How so? Is so? How not so? Not so *so!* There is no thing that is not acceptable. Sprouts rise up, and mighty pillars, lepers and lovely women, strange and extraordinary things—in Tao they are one. To divide One is to "accomplish," and whatever is accomplished is destruction; whatever is unaccomplished cannot be destroyed: it is eternally beginning again at the beginning, One. Only those who have arrived know this coming-again-into-One. They do not make use of their knowledge but dwell in the diurnal, and every day is what is used. Who uses it, understands it. Who understands gets all that's needed—and time—and *this is all.* When one relies on this alone and doesn't know it's so, that is Tao.

To exhaust the spirit and the mind by laboring to make things One, never realizing that they are all the same—I call this "Three in the morning." Why "Three in the morning"? There was a monkey keeper who fed his monkeys nuts. When he said, "I'll feed you three in the morning and four in the afternoon," the monkeys were furious. So he suggested, "Four in the morning and three in the afternoon," much to the monkeys' delight. The words say the same thing, and yet one phrasing produced anger, another delight. The keeper simply made use of this knowledge. The sage brings what *is* into harmony with right-and-wrong and rests under the tree of the balance of nature. This is called going two ways at once.

The ancients' knowledge was complete. How complete? There were some who refused to acknowledge that there were *things*. That complete. Nothing could be added to that. Then came some who acknowledged the existence of things but refused to discriminate among them; then some who discriminated but refused to label one "right" and another "wrong"; then right and

12

wrong became matters of adjudication and Tao became deficient; and because Tao became deficient, those who loved the Tao came to attempt to "accomplish" things. But are there really such things as "accomplishment" and "deficiency," or are there not?

There are. As when Chao Wen played the lute. And there are not. As when Chao Wen did not play the lute. Chao Wen's lute, music master Kuang and his baton, Hui Tzu leaning on the Wu tree: how much these three learned! All so mastered their respective arts that we still remember them today. What they cared for they differentiated, they made a "that" of it. What they cared for they desired to illuminate, but that was not the illumination of enlightenment. So we are left with Hui Tzu's obscure arguments about "hardness" and "whiteness" and Wen's disciples who ran out his string—and their own as well—and accomplished nothing. Or perhaps they did accomplish something. If so, so have I. And if this is not "accomplishment," then neither "things" nor I have ever accomplished anything.

For this reason, blazing chaos is the light that guides the sage. Rather than merely using things, the sage dwells in the ordinary. This may be called illumination.

NOW I WANT TO SAY A FEW WORDS. WHETHER THEY ARE THE right or wrong kind of words, they are at least some kind of words, and are no different than the words of others, so they're just okay. But please permit me to say them. There is a beginning. And there is a not-yet-beginning-to-be-a-beginning. There is a not-yet-beginning-to-be-a-not-yet-beginning-to-be-a-beginning. There is being. There is not beginning to be being. There is not yet beginning to be not yet beginning to be being. Oh, suddenly there's being and not being. Now I just had my say. But I don't know whether my saying has said anything or nothing. In All-under-heaven, there's nothing bigger than the tip of a dust mote floating in clear autumn air, and yet a mountain is a tiny thing. No one is older than the stillborn child, and twelve-hundred-year-old P'eng Tzu died young. Heaven and earth were born with me. The ten thousand things and I make one.

Now there's the One, and that's it, so how can I have said all that? But if I had said only, "Now there's the One, and that's it," would I not be saying something? The One and my saying make two; two and the One make three. Going on like this, even the most clever calculationist would never be done with it! Much less the rest of us. So: if by going from nothing to something we arrive at three, how much more might we get by going from something to something?

Don't be going from anywhere to anywhere. *Here is where it is!*

Before Tao was subjected to discriminations, words had not yet come to have precise definitions. But once "right" was distinguished, boundaries became defined. Let me say this about boundaries: there is a left and a right; there is sorting and assessment; there is division and discrimination; there is competition and conflict—the philosophers called these the Eight Virtues! Beyond the Six Realms, the sage embodies childlike clarity: he doesn't try to sort things out. Within the Six Realms, he sorts, but does not assess. On the true motives of former emperors as they are presented in the *Annals* and *Classics*, he assesses, but does not discriminate. There are things the dividers cannot divide, things discriminators cannot discriminate.

"What things?"—the sage embraces things, though throngs of men discriminate among them and make a great show of their discrimination. Therefore I say, "Those who discriminate cannot see."

The Great Tao has no title. Great discrimination has no words. Great compassion is not compassionate. Great modesty is reserved. Great courage is not aggressive. The Tao that shines forth is not Tao. Discriminating words never reach their mark. Compassion may be constant and yet accomplish nothing. Purity may be met with disbelief. Aggressive courage gets nothing done. These five fall within the circle, but tend to wander off . . .

Therefore: he who knows enough to stop at what he does not know is *there*. That's all. Who knows the wordless explanation and Tao that is not Tao? Know this and become the Storehouse of Heaven: where things may be put but never fill; where things may be taken yet never depleted. Yet he himself does not know why or how. He will be called the Pao-kuang Star, tip of the Dipper's handle, forever cycling slowly around the center, predicting coming seasons.

M<small>R</small>. C<small>HIPPED</small> T<small>OOTH</small> <small>QUESTIONED</small> W<small>ANG</small> N<small>I</small>, "Y<small>OU</small> <small>KNOW</small> what all things consider right, right?"

Wang Ni replied, "How should I know?"

"Well, you know what you *don't* know, don't you?"

Wang Ni replied, "How should I know?"

"So nothing knows anything?"

"How should I know? Although that's how it is, I'll try nevertheless to explain. If I say I understand, how can I know whether I don't know what I say I understand? If I say I don't understand, by what measure may I know that what I say I don't know I actually know? Let me ask: When people sleep wet, they catch pneumonia and die. Is that equally so of fish? If one were to try to live in a tree, one would be constantly fearful, but is that true of a monkey? Of the three, who knows the right place to live? People eat meat from animals who feed of hay and grain. Deer eat grass. Centipedes think snake tastes sweet. Owls and crows eat rats. Of the four, who knows which is the right flavor? Monkeys mate with monkeys, bucks with doe, fish with fish. All men consider Mao Chiang and Lady Li to be eternal beauties, but when fish see them, they dive quickly to the bottom; when birds see them, they fly off; and when deer see them, they bolt and run. Of the four, who knows right beauty here beneath the sky? As I see it, the lines of compassion and rectitude, the paths of right and wrong, are so knotted and gnarled that I can find no way to discriminate among them."

Chipped Tooth asked, "If you can't tell profit from loss, can the one who has 'gotten there' tell?"

Wang Ni replied, "The one who's 'gotten there' is a spirit being. If the Great Swamp dried up and burned, he wouldn't feel the heat; if the great river froze, he wouldn't feel the chill; if fierce explosions sundered the mountains and storms disrupted the seas, he wouldn't even be startled. It's his nature to rise on clouds in the air and straddle sun and moon, to wander beyond the four enclosing seas. Neither life nor death can change him, so how could puny things like profit and loss affect him?"

Chu the Magpie said to Mr. Tall Wu Tree, "The great master says he does not take charge of worldly affairs; he neither pursues profit nor avoids loss. He doesn't enjoy seeking. He isn't married to the Tao. He makes pronouncements without speaking; speaking, he says nothing. He rambles beyond the dirt and dust of this world. Master Kung, Confucius himself, took these to be bold, outrageous words. But I think that's how it is when you travel the mysterious Tao. What do you think?"

Mr. Tall Wu Tree said, "Even the Yellow Emperor would have gotten heated up hearing those words. How could Master Kung understand them? And you! You're getting way ahead of yourself, looking at eggs and expecting them to crow at sunrise, looking at a crossbow bolt and seeing roast dove on a spit. I'll talk a little crazy to you. See whether you can't listen a little crazy too. Leaning on sun and moon, the whole universe of space and time tucked neatly under one arm, he makes his marriage with whirling chaos. He honors the lowest of the low as his equal. While the struggling masses slave away at worldly tasks, the sage remains a simple rustic, ten thousand harvests his only accomplishment. Simple, pure, he sees the ten thousand things become simply *so*, and they form one whole."

How am I to know that this life is not merely a delusion? How am I to know that to despise death is not merely to be like one exiled in his youth and who now can find no way home? Beautiful Lady Li was the daughter of a petty knight of Ai. When

Chin first got her, she drenched the whole front of her gown with tears. But once she arrived at the palace and shared the emperor's bed and feasted on his fatted calves, she regretted her tears. How do I know that the dead do not regret clinging so ignominiously to life? Who dreams of drinking the wine of luxury may wake weeping in the sunrise. Who dreams of weeping may at dawn take up the hunt. As they dreamed, they didn't know that they were dreaming. Or in the midst of dreams they may have tried to find an omen in their dream. Awakened, they knew they'd been dreaming. Now, maybe there's a Great Big Awakening, after which we know that this has all been a Great Big Dream. Fools think they're awake now, having ferreted out the knowledge for themselves, on the sly, that this is so. One a lord; one a shepherd . . . Oh, sure!

Your Master Kung and you are both dreaming. And my saying you're both dreaming is also a dream. The name for all this is the Pitiful Deception. Ten thousand years from now, you may meet with a great sage who will know how to unravel this mystery for you. Or maybe you will this morning. Or this evening.

Suppose you and I have engaged in some dispute. If you won and I didn't, does that make you right and me wrong? If I won instead, does that make me right and you wrong? Is one of us right, the other wrong? Are both of us right or wrong? We can't agree. And no one else has even heard the argument yet. Who can straighten us out? If we pick someone who thinks like you, he'll agree with you; if we pick someone who thinks like me, he'll agree with me. If we pick someone who disagrees with both of us, his solution will certainly be disagreeable to both of us. He can't straighten things out. And someone who agrees with both of us won't help either. If neither you nor I nor anyone else can come to agreement, shall we wait around for yet another opinion?

Or perhaps we should find the harmony in the origin of all things? It's said, "Is and is not; so and not so. If *is* fits things and *isn't* doesn't, then *is* and *isn't* differ, and there is no dispute. If *so* is true of things, then there's no disputing it's different from *not so.*" The alternating noises of dispute await their turns, but you

17

need not attend them. Harmonize them with the beginning of all things and move on the endless flow until you exhaust your years. Forget years! Forget judgments! Flap your wings and fly to the palace without boundaries and live there!

The shade asked the shadow, "A while ago you were moving. Now you've stopped. A while ago you were sitting and now you rise. How is it that you have no particular place to be, nothing particular to do?"

The shadow asked in reply, "Am I supposed to wait for something before I do what I do? Is the something I'm supposed to wait for waiting for something also? Shall I wait for snake skin or cicada wings? And how would I know if that's so? How could I know if it wasn't?"

LONG AGO, CHUANG CHOU DREAMED HE WAS A BUTTERFLY fluttering among trees, doing as he pleased, completely unaware of a Chuang Chou. A sudden awakening, and there, looking a little out of sorts, was Chuang Chou. Now, I don't know whether it is Chou who dreamed he was a butterfly, or whether a butterfly dreams he's Chuang Chou. But between Chuang Chou and the butterfly, we ought to be able to find some sort of distinction. This is what's known as Things Changing.

Nurturing Life

[CHAPTER 3]

L IFE HAS A LIMIT; KNOWLEDGE HAS NONE. TO SEEK WHAT is limitless through what is limited is perilous. It is even more perilous to pursue knowledge with full knowledge of this fact. Those
who would do good should avoid fame just as those who do evil
would avoid punishment. Make staying close to main arteries a
constant rule. Doing so, you may remain whole, rear a family, and
live out all your days.

Ting the cook was cutting meat free from the bones of an ox for
Lord Wen-hui. His hands danced as his shoulders turned with the
step of his foot and bending of his knee. With a shush and a hush,
the blade sang following his lead, never missing a note. Ting and
his blade moved as though dancing to "The Mulberry Grove," or
as if conducting the "Ching-shou" with a full orchestra.

Lord Wen-hui exclaimed, "What a joy! It's good, is it not, that
such a simple craft can be so elevated?"

Ting laid aside his knife. "All I care about is the Way. I find it in my craft, that's all. When I first butchered an ox, I saw nothing but ox meat. It took three years for me to see the whole ox. Now I go out to meet it with my whole spirit and don't think only about what meets the eye. Sensing and knowing stop. The spirit goes where it will, following the natural contours, revealing large cavities, leading the blade through openings, moving onward according to actual form—yet not touching the central arteries or tendons and ligaments, much less touching bone.

"A good cook need sharpen his blade but once a year. He cuts cleanly. An awkward cook sharpens his knife every month. He chops. I've used this knife for nineteen years, carving thousands of oxen. Still the blade is as sharp as the first time it was lifted from the whetstone. At the joints there are spaces, and the blade has no thickness. Entering with no thickness where there is space, the blade may move freely where it will: there's plenty of room to move. Thus, after nineteen years, my knife remains as sharp as it was that first day.

"Even so, there are always difficult places, and when I see rough going ahead, my heart offers proper respect as I pause to look deeply into it. Then I work slowly, moving my blade with increasing subtlety until—kerplop!—meat falls apart like a crumbling clod of earth. I then raise my knife and assess my work until I'm fully satisfied. Then I give my knife a good cleaning and put it carefully away."

Lord Wen-hui said, "That's good, indeed! Ting the cook has shown me how to find the Way to nurture life."

⤳

WHEN KUNG-WEN HSIEN SAW THE COMMANDER OF THE Right, he exclaimed, "Who can this be? How is it he has but one foot? Is this a gift of nature or an amputation, a punishing gift of men?"

"This is natural," he was told, "not the doing of men. He was born with just one foot. He is gifted with the appearance of great dignity. That's how we know it is natural."

20

⤢

THE MARSH PHEASANT WILL GO TEN STEPS FOR A SINGLE peck of food and a hundred for a single sip of water, but you can't beg him into eating once he's caged. Though he may be a king in spirit, it does no good.

⤢

WHEN LAO TZU DIED, CHIN SHIH CAME TO MOURN. HE uttered three loud cries and went out. A disciple said, "You're no friend of our master, are you?"

"I am so."

"If that's so, how can you mourn in this manner?"

"I mourn as I mourn," Chin Shih replied. "At first, I took *you* to be his men, but now I do not. When I went in to mourn, old folks were wailing as if for their own children and young folks wailing as if over their mothers. What is it that brought these people together? Certainly they have words to say and tears to cry that no one begged them for. But this is only hiding from true nature, turning one's back to actuality. In the old days, they called this 'hiding from the lessons of nature.'

"The master came, knowing his season. When it went, he followed. He is gone with his season, gone where he is supposed to go. Joys and sorrows cannot enter there. In the old days, this was called 'being cut free from bondage.'"

⤢

LOOK! THERE'S NO NEED FOR MORE KINDLING. THE FIRE burns on. It knows no end.

21

In the Human World

[CHAPTER 4]

YEN HUI WENT TO SEE CONFUCIUS BEFORE TAKING leave.

"Where to?"

"To Wei," Hui replied.

"And why are you going there?"

"I've heard something about the Prince of Wei: he's reached maturity and is very independent. But he's irresponsible in his governance, refusing to see his own excesses. He is particularly irresponsible toward the common people, who are dying in such great numbers that his land looks like a drought-struck marsh. And there's nothing they can do.

"I've often heard you say, 'When a country is well governed, you may leave it; where there is chaos, you must go.' Now there are many suffering people waiting outside the doctor's door. I want to use what I've learned from you to help heal the illness of that land."

22

Confucius said, "That would be nice. But very dangerous. You'll more likely end up suffering punitive mutilation for all your trouble. You'll likely lose an ear, at least. The Tao must not be complicated. Where there is complication, there's multiplicity; where there is multiplicity, you're close to grief already; and when you've come to grief, there's no hope of saving you. Those among the ancients who truly *got there* did it by learning to be masters of the child within themselves, and only then did they try to care for the children of others. You've not yet mastered caring for yourself; how can you expect to master a tyrant?

"What's more," Confucius said, "you must understand that the Power of Virtue may go floating off and mere knowledge may take its place. Virtue can float away in search of fame and honor, while knowledge arises from conflict. Fame and honor can be armor, and knowledge a weapon of war. Both are instruments of evil. They're not the tools you need to do your work.

"The power of your virtue is strong," he continued, "as is your will to goodness. But you don't yet fully understand the true nature of humanity. Although you resist contending for honors, you don't yet see deeply into the hearts and minds of men. If you appear before this tyrant to urge his use of the Carpenter's Plumb Line of Humanity and Righteousness, you will merely make an evil man despise you for your very goodness. He'll charge you with injuring his reputation; he'll say you mouth evil and quote, 'Who speaks evil of others will have evil done against himself.' The man you courageously go to face will do you evil.

"Or suppose on the other hand that he was the sort who takes pleasure in the good and wouldn't countenance evil—then there'd be no use in trying to change him, would there?

"Better not preach there at all," Confucius said. "A king or a duke is likely to take advantage of your counsel to show off his dominance with a witty chiding. Then your eyes will burn and you'll turn pale as you try to pacify him. Your mouth will work at placating him, your face will twist into false expressions while your heart and mind struggle to find an angle from which to agree with his arguments. This is called fighting fire with fire.

Or water with more of the same. I call it the full benefit of multiplicity!

"And once you've given him the lead, there'll be no end to it.
You'll be in danger of losing your own goodness under a heap of
verbiage. Then you will die before your tyrant.

"Long ago, Chieh murdered Kuan Lung-feng and Chou murdered Prince Pi Kan. Both Kuan and the prince were men inclined
toward the comforts of their people, yet who stood firm before the
power of their lords. But because they loved fame and honors too
much, their overlords bent their very strengths back against them.

"In ancient times," Confucius continued, "Yao attacked Tsung-
chih and Hsu-ao, and Yu attacked Yu-hu. Those lands lay deso-
late, and those lords' own bodies suffered punitive mutilation.
They had waged war incessantly in search of material gain. All of
these were seekers after honors and material gain. Surely you
knew of them? Not even the sages Yao and Yu could bring such
minions of fame and gain to heel peacefully.

"Be that as it may, you must have a plan. Tell me."

Yen Hui said, "I will be principled and selfless, constrained and
unified in purpose. Will that do?"

"It will *not* do. The prince is full of yang and loves to show off.
He's inclined toward pleasures of the flesh and is very unstable.
Ordinary people dare deny him nothing. He takes from others
what they hold most dear in order to force their submission to his
will. Can't you see? He is incapable of practicing even the most
simple, ordinary manners. Is it likely he'll find the Power of True
Virtue? He will cling to his own ways, refusing to change. He may
outwardly accept your advice, but inwardly he will not. How
could such a vulgar course lead to success?"

"Well then," Yen Hui replied, "what if I'm inwardly straight
but outwardly crooked, and whatever I do, I support it by citing
the precedents of the ancients? Whoever is straight within is a
companion of nature. Whoever is a companion of nature is a Son
of Heaven and knows that he and the emperor are both Sons of
Heaven equally. So I would have no need to seek praise for the
'goodness' of my words, nor any fear of reproach. If I can act just

so, people will call me an innocent child. That is what I mean by being a companion of nature.

"Those who are crooked on the outside are the companions of men. Bowing and scraping, making the body crooked, these are merely the good manners of ministers at court. Men all act this way. Who does as others do avoids blame. This is what I mean by being the companion of men. And supporting whatever I do by citing the ancients is simply being a companion of the ancients. Although my words may instruct or reprimand, they are the words of the ancients, not my own. If I manage things just so, although I am upright, I will not be blamed. This is what I mean by being a companion of the ancients. If I can be just so, will that work?"

"It will *not*," Confucius replied. "It will not work. You have here a grand multiplicity of methods, none of which is really appropriate. If you manage to stay firmly within them, you may wiggle your way out of mutilation, but even so, that's as far as you'll get. What's to get him to change? In your heart, you're still too much the preacher."

"I can't get any farther," Yen Hui said. "May I ask what methods you'd employ?"

"Fast," Confucius said, "and then I'll tell you. But having the method is one thing, carrying it out is another. Will it be easy? Whoever thinks it might be easy is surely unsuited to the task."

"My family is practically penniless," Yen Hui said. "I haven't tasted wine or spiced meat in months. Does that count as fasting?"

"That's fasting for a sacrifice, not the fasting of heart and mind."

"May I ask then about the fasting of heart and mind?"

"Set your heart and mind on the One," Confucius replied. "Don't listen with your ear; listen with your heart and mind. Then stop listening with your heart and mind and listen with your *ch'i*, the very energy of your being. Hearing stops with the ear. Heart and mind stop with words and symbols. The *ch'i* is empty. Being so, it is able to attend upon all phenomena. Tao comes to roost in emptiness. This emptiness is the fasting of the mind."

When next they met, Yen Hui said, "Before I tried it, I was still Hui. Now that I've gotten it, I'm not sure there's a beginning to be a Hui. Is this what you call emptiness?"

"The whole thing." Confucius paused. "Now I can say to you, you may enter and go rambling around in that cage of his and yet remain untouched by fame and honors. If the prince calls you to an audience, sing like a bird. If he does not, be silent. Where there is no gate, no evil can enter. Make the One your home and dwell there when there's nothing else you can do. Then you'll be close to really being there. To stop leaving tracks is easy; but to walk without touching the ground is difficult. In the service of men, it's easy to be false; in the service of nature, it's difficult. You have heard of flying with wings, but never of flying without them. You have heard of those who know with knowledge, but never of the knowing that is without knowledge. In the empty chamber, the light lives on. There, good fortune and blessings stop and remain still. And if *you* don't stop, that's what's called meditating on horseback—where the body sits while the mind races on. If you keep eye and ear connected to what's inside, and keep heart and mind and knowledge outside, the very spirits of earth and air will throng to dwell within you, and how much more will mere men then be drawn to you? This is the ten thousand things, ever-changing. It is the bond shared by Yu and Shun, the practice of Fu Hsi and Chi Ch'u from beginning to end. And how much more does it deserve to be spread among ordinary people?"

THE DUKE OF SHE, TZU KAO, WAS ABOUT TO DEPART ON A mission to the state of Ch'i. He consulted Confucius, saying, "The king has charged me with a heavy responsibility. Ch'i will most likely make a great show of respect but be in no hurry to do anything more. You can't just push even an ordinary man into doing things. How much more true must that be when one is

dealing with a feudal lord? I'm deeply afraid. You've often told me
that whether the affair is great or small, except by following the
Tao, few reach full completion. If you don't achieve your goal,
you'll suffer gossip. If you do, you'll suffer from the inevitable
shifting balance of yin and yang. The ability to *not suffer*, regardless of succeeding or not succeeding—only the possessor of the
Power of Virtue can attain that. You know I eat only plain food, so
there's no need for cooling remedies in my larder. Well, this
morning I received my orders, and this evening I'm drinking ice
water. It's as if my insides were cooking. I haven't even got to the
substance of my task yet and I'm already suffering from the im-
balance of yin and yang! If I fail, everyone will condemn me. As a
minister, I just don't have sufficient footing to undertake this embassy. Is there something you can tell me?"

"In All-under-heaven," Confucius replied, "there are but two
Great Precepts: one is destiny, the other duty. That a child loves
its parents is destiny: there is no cutting free of heart and mind
from this. That a minister must serve his sovereign is duty: there
is no place you can go, no place you can flee to in this world of
men where there is no ruler. Thus these are called the Great
Precepts.

"To serve your parents willingly and to dwell wherever they
choose is the ultimate goal in filial devotion. In serving one's lord,
to accept whatever charge one is given and go wherever it leads—
that is truly fulsome loyalty. To serve your own heart and mind
so that neither sadness nor joy comes too easily to the fore, to
know what you can't change and accept it as destined—that is
getting on toward the Power of Virtue.

"Whoever serves another as a minister of state," Confucius
said, "will often fail to gain his own satisfaction. He will do what
is actually to be done, and forget himself. What time will he have
for loving life or hating death? I think you are ready for that sort
of service now.

"But I have something else to tell you, too. Whenever relations
are between those who live close to each other, there will be mutual trust on the basis of physical familiarity. But if they dwell at

some distance apart, loyalty will depend on language, and words must be passed on by *someone*. Whether words are pleasing to both sides or whether they are angering, this can be one of the most difficult tasks in the world. If the message is mutually pleasing, there will be a tendency to pretty it up. If the message stirs anger, there'll be a tendency to exaggerate the conflict. Whatever even appears exaggerated in any way is foolish and reckless. Where there is recklessness, will there be trust? When there is no trust, even the messenger is in danger. That's why the *Fa-yen* says, 'Communicate the plain facts; don't embellish them when you speak.' Follow that advice, and you'll get out whole.

"When men test one another at martial feats, things always start out sunny bright yang, but often quickly turn cloudy dark yin, and then they bring all their most devious arts to bear. Like men who begin drinking wine in full accord with ceremony, they start out in good order but all too soon begin to be disorderly. And they usually end up with all sorts of lewdness. So it goes with other affairs as well," Confucius continued. "What begins in sincerity may end up in duplicity. What begins small and simple may become large and complicated before it's through. The speaker is like a man on stormy waters: his course may lead to success or to doom. Stormy waters move with changes. Success and failure walk the cliff's edge of change as well. Thus anger may seem to arise without cause. First there may be clever speeches and slanted phrases, then, like wild beasts squealing, shrieking in rage, roaring in death throes, all raw and unformed their very *ch'i* may come rushing out. Once both sides are enraged, the seeds of destruction are close at hand.

"Response and rejoinder will come from hearts and minds made inhuman, and they themselves won't even know that it is so. When you act without knowing why you are acting, who can tell where things will end? That's why the *Fa-yen* says, 'Don't stray from orders. Don't press for a quick conclusion. Going beyond these limits is going to excess. Going beyond your commission to reach a settlement is a dangerous thing.' A nice job may take time. A bad job may take forever to repair. Can you be otherwise than careful? Just take advantage of things as they are. Let your heart and mind roam free. Accept what you can't get and nourish your center on that acceptance. Then you're there. That's all. What else is required? Nothing but that you be willing to act in accord with your own destiny, even if that means going to your death. This is the only difficulty."

⌣⌒

WHEN YEN HO WAS ABOUT TO BECOME TUTOR TO THE Crown Prince, son of Duke Ling of Wei, he went to seek counsel from Ch'u Po-yu, saying, "We have one here who seems to be a natural-born killer. If I can't bring him to heel, I fear for the whole country; but if I try to bring him to heel, I'll be walking the edge of the precipice myself. He knows enough to recognize the faults of others, but not enough to recognize his own. This being so, what can I do?"

"Good question," Ch'u Po-yu replied. "Go well armed with caution. Make yourself just like a woman, let your form conform while heart and mind find harmony. And although it may be handled just so, there is still a present danger, as with dual loyalties. Don't let your conformity become too deeply internalized nor let your inner harmony become too apparent or you'll fall into certain ruin, you'll crumble and perish. If your inner harmony becomes too obvious, you'll be talked about, and as your fame grows so will your blame, and you will eventually be seen as evil. If he acts like a child, play the child with him. If he sees no boundaries, see no boundaries. If he recklessly wanders cliffside trails, climb with him, leading him toward a place where carelessness does not exist.

"You've no doubt heard the story of the praying mantis who, enraged, spread its arms to stop the approaching chariot in its track. He didn't have a chance. So it is with anyone so vain about his talents. Go well armed with caution. Making a great display will only offend him, and you'll make a mantis of yourself.

"Do you know about tiger keepers? They wouldn't dare feed

their tigers a living animal for fear of them getting a taste for the kill. Nor do they feed the tigers whole animals, for tearing apart the carcass engenders tigers' fury. Feed them well in a timely fashion and you can take the heart right out of the tiger's rage, making it your slave. Tigers and people differ, but both cherish those who feed and care for them. Tigers kill only those who oppose them.

"There was a horse lover who collected his horse's dung in a fancy box and its piss in a big clay jar. When a fly lit on his horse, he slapped it. Surprised, the horse bolted, breaking its bit, injuring its head and banging its chest. Despite his intentions to achieve perfect affection for his horse, the horse lover caused harm. Can we be other than cautious?"

⌣

A WOODWORKER NAMED STONE TRAVELED TO CH'I. WHEN he got to Ch'u-yuan, he saw a great chestnut tree that served as a village shrine. Large enough to shade thousands of oxen, it was a hundred spans around and rose high as a mountain, it lowest branches some eighty feet above the ground. More than a dozen of these lower branches were large enough to be hollowed out into boats. Sightseers were packed together like at the marketplace. Woodworker Stone barely gave it a glance, continuing along his way without looking back. But his apprentices couldn't keep from gawking, then had to run to catch up. One said, "Since we took up our axes to follow you, Master, we've never seen such beautiful material. But you didn't give it a second look! You went right on by. How can this be?"

"Enough!" Stone cried. "Don't talk about it. That wood is trash. Make a boat from it and the boat will sink. For coffins, it rots too fast. For utensils, it's too brittle. It seeps too much sap to use for a gate or door. Make a pillar, and it will attract worms. It's not good timber for anything. It can't be used. That's how it got so old."

After the woodworker returned home, the great tree appeared

30

to him in a dream, saying, "You compare me to cultivated trees, the hawthorne, the pear, the orange, all the shrubs and trees that bear fruit? When their fruit is ripe they're stripped, peeled, and generally abused, big branches broken off, little ones dripping sap from wounds. They have a wonderful ability to make a miserable life of usefulness. The string of their days and years cut off, they are beaten and torn up by unruly saps. So it is for all things in the world. That's why I strive to master the arts of uselessness. Although it nearly killed me, I've got it now. It's really useful to me. If I were of any use, do you suppose there'd be any chance for me to have grown so large? You and I are both *things*. Why pass judgment? You're a man born to die. Are you mere trash? Why call me trash?"

When the woodworker Stone awakened, he told his apprentices about his dream.

"If it's trying so hard to be useless, why has it become a shrine?" they wanted to know.

"That's a secret," Stone replied. "Don't mention it to anyone. It's just pretending. This way it can also be protected from people who don't appreciate uselessness. If it weren't portraying a shrine, it might still be cut down and cut up. It hides its difference from others. You might honor it for the nobility of its intentions, but that might be going a bit too far."

THE CHINGSHIH DISTRICT OF THE STATE OF SUNG IS PERfectly suited to growing catalpa, cypress, and mulberry trees. Once they are a span or two around, people cut them for monkey perches. When they make it to three or four spans, they're cut for fancy ridgepoles. Those surviving to seven or eight spans get cut to make sideboards for the coffins of nobility and the very rich. Therefore they never live out their allotted days and years, but fall to the ax along the way. This is the calamity that comes from having material value.

White blazed oxen, pigs with upturned snouts, and men with

hemorrhoids may not be offered in the River Sacrifices. All priests know this and consider them all "unlucky creatures." The True Spirit Being, however, calls them "the great good luckies"!

The man called Crippled Tree has his chin in his belly button, his shoulders hunched above his head, neck bone pointing at the sky. His five major organs are all on top, two thigh bones against his ribs. He does needlework and laundry for his food, and by rewinnowing chaff for grain makes enough to feed ten people. When they call for conscription, his crippled body rambles at leisure, and when there's a community labor party, since he's listed among the chronically ill, he never makes muster. When they pass out welfare grain, he gets three full measures along with ten loads of firewood. His *form* is crippled, to be sure, but still sufficient to his need. Surely, he'll run out the full string of his years. How much more so will be the case of those with crippled virtue?

CONFUCIUS TRAVELED TO CH'U. THE MADMAN OF CH'U, Chieh Yu, came rambling up to his gate and cried, "Phoenix! Oh, Phoenix! What's to be done as virtue's power wanes? You can't wait for the next generation and you can't have back the ones who've gone. When All-under-heaven follows the Tao, the sage does sage deeds. But when the world is without the Way, the sage survives in it. The method for this season is to stop before facing mutilation. Good fortune is light, yet none know how to put on its wings. Misfortune is heavy as earth and no one can escape it. Oh, be done! Be done with drawing people on by the power of your virtue! It's dangerous, very dangerous to mark the Way in the dust so as to set people running. False light! There is no injury in my way of going. My tracks run crooked, but they don't hurt my feet. The mountain tree is self-plundering, the fat fuels its own fire. Cinnamon is edible, so they cut it down. The lacquer tree is useful, so they hack at it. Everyone knows the use of usefulness; nobody understands the usefulness of the useless."

The Sign and Seal of the Power of Virtue Standing on Its Own Two Feet

[CHAPTER 5]

I N THE STATE OF LU THERE WAS A MAN NAMED WANG T'AI who, despite having lost a foot to punitive mutilation, traveled with a following as great as that of Confucius himself. Ch'ang Chi asked Confucius about it. "Wang T'ai had a foot cut off and yet his followers split Lu right down the middle with your followers. When he stands up, he doesn't preach, and when he sits, he doesn't discuss. Nevertheless, they come to him empty and go home full. It seems that although his form is incomplete, he has a wordless teaching, his heart and mind complete. What sort of man *is* this?"

Confucius answered, "This gentleman is a true sage. If I haven't visited him yet, it's only because I'm a little backward. I'm going to make him my master. How much more should those who are not my equal be so inclined? And how could this apply to the state of Lu alone? I shall lead All-under-heaven to follow in his footsteps."

"That man had a foot chopped off," Ch'ang Chi said, "and yet you accept him as your teacher. Certainly his practice is far indeed from the Mean. And his method of using heart and mind—in what way is it unique?"

"Life and death are great issues," Confucius replied, "yet they mark no change for him. If heaven and earth were overthrown and fell, he wouldn't take it as a loss. He judges without pretense and remains unmoved by mere phenomena. He accepts change while guarding the source of origins."

"What do you mean?" Ch'ang Chi asked.

"Looking from the point of view of difference," Confucius said, "the liver and the gall bladder are as far apart as the states of Ch'u and Yueh. Looking from the point of view of similarity, all the ten thousand things are the One. This gentleman is so in tune with *suchness* that he doesn't even know what the eyes and ears are *for*. He rambles, heart and mind in harmony with the Power of Virtue. He sees all things as one and so he never stands with his eyes on what he has lost. He sees the loss of his own foot as a legacy to the earth."

"He's done it!" Ch'ang Chi exclaimed. "He's used his knowledge to get to his heart and mind, and his heart and mind to get to the Constant Heart and Mind. But why is it that things are so attracted to him?"

"No one uses running water for a mirror," Confucius replied. "Rather we gaze into still water. Only the still can instill a single stillness in the rushing many. Of all that draw their lives from the earth below, only pine and cypress, cemetery trees, remain so still. Summer and winter, forever green. Of all those who have taken their lives from the sky above, only Yao and Shun could stay still at the One. What good fortune that they could make their lives so upright and thus rectify the lives of the many!

"Drawing upon the forces of birth and bringing them to fruition in fearlessness, a single warrior may crow like a cock as he stands alone against the Nine Armies. If one can—in a mere quest for fame and the gratification of one's own desires—become like this, how much more might one become who puts heaven and earth in order, houses all things, treats his own body as no more than a dwelling place, understands that perceptions of eye and ear are mere images, and knows all that is knowable as the One? The heart and mind of this one will never die. He will choose the day to rise and go and the people will follow. Yet to the marrow of his bones, he will be unwilling to serve mere things."

⌒

SHEN-T'U CHIA, A FORMER OFFICIAL, HAD LOST A FOOT TO puni-tive amputation. Along with Tzu-ch'an, who later became Prime Minister of the state of Cheng, he was studying with Master Po-hun Wu-jen. Tzu-ch'an spoke to Shen-t'u, saying, "If I go out first, you stay put. If you go out first, I'll stay put."

The next day they were again meditating on the same mat in the same hall when Tzu-ch'an said, "When I go, you stay put; when you go, I stay put. I'm going out now. Will you stay? Or aren't you ready yet? Of course you have seen prime ministers be-fore and have shown no awe. Do you think yourself the equal of a prime minister?"

Shen-t'u replied, "Within our master's gates, is there really such a thing as a prime minister? You delight in stepping on oth-ers in order to make yourself a prime minister. I heard a saying: 'If the mirror is bright, it is because no dirt has settled on it. Where dirt stays on it, the mirror is not bright. If you stay put with a worthy teacher, you may learn to be without error.' Now you re-gard our master as a worthy man, yet utter such words! Isn't there an error here somewhere?"

Tzu-ch'an said, "You, such a one! And still you think you can compete with the sage Yao in goodness. Consider the power of your virtue! Have you any footing at all to take such a stand here?"

Shen-t'u answered, "Those who excuse their errors and claim they didn't deserve the loss are a multitude. Those who refuse to

35

excuse their error or claim they didn't deserve to remain intact—these are very few. To know that about which nothing can be done and to accept it peacefully, as destined—only those with the power of virtue can do this. If you ramble around in front of the great archer Yi's target, when you are right on the bull's eye, you'll *be* the bull's eye. If you don't get hit, that's destiny.

"Many people in good standing laugh at us footless ones. It makes me boil with an angry heart and mind. Then I come to our master's place and it all burns itself out, and then I can go home again. I don't know whether the master has washed me clean; I know only that I've traveled with him through nineteen years and he hasn't yet acknowledged any lack of standing on my part. Now you and I are here to ramble about states deep within our forms and bodies, and yet you want to tie me to mere externals. Isn't that an error?"

Tzu-ch'an, realizing that he was the one without a leg to stand on, changed color and expression and said, "Say no more."

⌒

IN LU THERE WAS A PENAL AMPUTEE CALLED NO-TOES SHU Shan who came stomping in for an interview with Confucius.

"You were careless in putting yourself forward," the sage observed. "You've already offended the authorities and suffered this calamity of the feet. What are you up to now?"

No-toes said, "It's just that I didn't know my duty then, and took my body too lightly. So, sure enough, I lost a foot. Now I've come here with enough of me left to provide sufficient footing to let me honor the body I was born with. As I see it, my duty is to remain whole. There's nothing the sky doesn't cover, nothing the earth doesn't bear. Master, I took you to be my sky and my earth. How could I have known you would treat me so?"

"I was rude," Confucius said. "Come in and let me tell you what I have heard."

No-toes left.

Confucius said, "My disciples, I commend this one to you. Mr.

36

No-toes has lost his feet to punitive amputation, and yet he recognizes his duty to study and to mend his former evil ways. How much more is it incumbent upon us, with our full powers still intact, to do so?"

～

No-toes said to Lao Tzu, "Well, now! As far as Confucius and his 'getting there' goes, *not quite yet*, eh? Where does he get off insinuating himself in here to study your Way? He's trying to carve out a reputation for himself as a famous and remarkable man, never realizing that one who's 'gotten there' takes things like that to be shackles and fetters."

Lao Tzu replied, "Why didn't you show him that life and death are a single strand, that may and may not are just two sides of a coin, and cut him free of his fetters? You might have."

"If heaven has bound him for punishment, how could *I* cut him free?"

～

Duke Ai of Lu questioned Confucius, "In Wei there was a truly ugly fellow called Horse-face Ai. When men got close to him, their thoughts were always on him, and they could never leave. When women saw him, they pleaded with their parents, 'Rather than becoming the head wife of any other man, I would be this man's concubine!' This has happened at least ten times already. And yet no one has ever heard him take the lead part. He always assumes the harmony behind the voices of others. He didn't have a government office that gave him the power of life and death over people, nor a full storehouse to appeal to people's bellies. And as I said, he was ugly enough to amaze All-under-heaven. All he did was sing harmony. He didn't know anything about anything, but right where he was. Yet men and women flocked together like geese around him.

"I thought he must be an extraordinary man, so I called for him

37

and had a look for myself. He was *frighteningly* ugly! But I kept him around, and it was barely a month before I began to get some idea of him as a man. In less than a year, he had my full faith. I had no chief minister then, so I offered him the reins of the state. Before answering, he moped around as if he were going to beg off, which made me feel ashamed. But I persisted and handed the government of my realm to him. Then, in no time at all, he simply left me. I was cut to the quick, as if I'd lost my very realm, as if there were no one with whom I could share the enjoyments of the kingdom. Just what sort of person was he?"

Confucius replied, "Once when I was on a mission in the state of Ch'u, I saw piglets suckling their dead mother. After a while, looking startled, they ran off. They could no longer see themselves, or even their own kind, in her. Love for the mother is not a matter of form; it is a matter of what creates that form. If a man dies in battle, he won't mind if he's buried without decorations. When a man has no feet, he has no reason to love shoes. In both cases, they have lost the root of love. That's a radical loss.

"Those who will be consorts of the Son of Heaven do not pare their nails or pierce their ears. A man who takes a wife is allowed to stay outside the court, freed from official duties. If a whole body is enough to put one on such a special footing, how much more exalted must be the position of one whose power of virtue is entirely intact?

"Now this Horse-face Ai of yours: before he spoke a word, men trusted his word. Without any merit earned, he was cherished. He caused people to hand over their states to him, their only fear being that he might decline. He must have been one whose talent was perfect, the power of whose virtue was without form."

"What do you mean by 'perfect talent'?" Duke Ai wanted to know.

"Death and life," Confucius said, "persisting and perishing, exhaustion and completion, poverty and wealth, worthiness and worthlessness, blame and praise, hunger and thirst, cold and heat—the alternation of these things is the work of destiny. Day and night, they roll on, and 'knowing' can't even see back to their birth. Therefore they haven't sufficient footing to muddle the harmony. There is nowhere for them in the storehouse of the spirit. Let your mind be in harmony. Take delight. Understand. Never let joy be lost, day or night, ceaselessly, eternally in the springtime of things, always connecting, making the very seasons come alive within your heart and mind. This is what I mean when I speak of perfect talent."

"What do you mean when you speak of the power of his virtue being without form?"

"At peace, like still water and its fullness. To go as water is the method. To keep guarded what is within, so that it is not easily ruffled by anything outside. The Power of Virtue lives in the accomplishment of such perfect harmony, and when the Power of Virtue is without form, nothing can be separate from it."

Later, Duke Ai spoke to Min Tzu about it. "I used to sit facing south and lord it over All-under-heaven," he said. "I held the reins of the people and was anxious for their lives. I thought I understood everything. Now that I've heard the words of someone who is really *there*, I'm afraid I didn't really have the facts. I was taking myself too lightly and threatening the state. Confucius and I are hardly lord and minister; we are friends by the Power of Virtue, and that's that."

CHUANG TZU SAID, "THERE WAS A HUNCHBACK CALLED Crippled No-lips who spoke to Duke Ling of Wei. Duke Ling took such great joy in his words that when he looked at normal people, he saw them stiff-backed and fat-lipped. A fellow with his neck swollen to the size of a jar spoke to Duke Huan of Ch'i, and the duke took such joy in his words that when he looked at normal people, he pitied their skinny necks. So: the Power of Virtue is what lasts, and mere form may be forgotten. That's sincere forgetting. So the sage wanders. Knowledge is a curse to him. All agreements are mere glue. Virtue is a grasping and skill is for commerce. He doesn't scheme. Why would he need knowledge?

39

He doesn't dismantle things, so why would he need glue? He's not separate from anything, so what would he grasp? He has no business, so what need of skill? In the place of these four qualities, he takes the gruel of heaven. The gruel of heaven is heaven's provision. Since he is fed by heaven, what use has he for humankind? He has human form, but no human feelings. Because he has the form, he goes with the herd. But since he has no human feelings, right and wrong have no hold on his body. Puny and small, he is truly only one among humans. Infinite and great, alone he is one with heaven."

Hui Tzu asked, "So there are humans with no feelings?"

"That's so."

"No feelings!" Hui Tzu repeated. "How can you call that a man?"

"The Tao provides his figure," Chuang Tzu said, "and heaven gives him form. How can you *not* call him a man?"

"If we call him human, how can he be without feelings?"

"You mistake what I mean by feelings," Chuang Tzu replied. "I say such a man doesn't permit good and bad to wound his body. He goes as nature goes, and seeks no benefit from life."

"If he takes no benefit from life, " Hui Tzu asked, "how can he have a body?"

"The Tao provides his figure, heaven his form. There is no good nor bad to harm his body," Chuang Tzu said. "You, now! You put your spirit aside and belabor your vital essence:

> "Leaning on your tree, you mumble;
> Propped on your desk, you doze.
> Heaven gave you form, all right,
> And you waste it all just warbling
> On and on about *hard* and *white*."

40

The Great Ancestral Teacher

[CHAPTER 6]

THOSE WHO KNOW HEAVEN AND KNOW HUMANKIND ARE there. Those who know heaven know heaven gives one life. Whoever knows humankind uses knowing to nurture what cannot be known. They will run out the string of their years and not find it cut off in the middle. This is the fullest knowledge. And yet, though this is so, there is a problem: knowledge waits on certainty, but certainty is never quite certain. How can I know that what I call "heaven" is not really "humankind," or that what I call "humankind" is not really "heaven"? Only when there is one who is truly human can there be True Knowledge.

What is a true human? The True Ones of antiquity didn't reject being solitary, didn't crow about accomplishments, and didn't lay plans. Just so! When they failed, they felt no regret. When they succeeded, they didn't grow self-satisfied. Just so! They climbed high without fear. They went into the water without sinking.

They went into fire without feeling the heat. This is how close
their knowledge had risen toward the Way.

The True Ones of antiquity slept without dreams and awakened without anxiety. They did not need to sweeten what they
ate. They breathed deep. The True One breathes from the heels;
ordinary people breathe from their throats.

The crooked retch up their words like vomit. In those whose
lusts are deep, the motion of heaven is shallow. The True Ones of
antiquity didn't know to take joy from life, didn't know to despise
death. Coming forth, they didn't rejoice; going back, they did not
resist. Gone suddenly on the wing, or coming on the wing, that's
all. Never forgetting the womb we spring from, they face the winter wherein their strings will end. Receiving and enjoying, forgetting and beginning again, this is what is called "not letting the
heart and mind devour the Way, not letting humankind 'help'
heaven." This is what I mean when I say, "True Human."

Because people are so, heart and mind let go, their faces grow
quiet, their brows calm. They are cool as autumn, warm as spring.
Knowing joy and anger like the circling seasons, people know the
potency of all things. There is no knowing their limits. Thus,
when the sage of old raised armies, he might lose his land, but
never the hearts and minds of his people. He anointed ten thousand generations with his bounty, but not merely for the affection
of the people.

Those who delighted in bringing success to things were not
sages. Those who felt affection were not truly benevolent. Those
who acted at the appointed times were not worthy. Those who
could not reconcile damage and advantage were not princes.
Those who lost their bodies in the search for fame were not
knights. And those who lost their bodies without regard for the
True? They weren't even fit to be lackeys. Famous men like Hu
Pu-hsieh, Wu Kuang, Po Yi, Shu Ch'i, Chi Tzu, Hsu Yu, Chi T'o
and Shen-t'u Ti were the lackeys of lackeys. They strove to
achieve others' ends, never achieving their own.

The True One of antiquity was a lonely peak standing apart
from the crumbling range, a solitary figure who didn't need to

form a "party." Seeming always to lack, the True One accepted nothing, standing four-square without being rigid, being plain rather than flashy, smiling as if happy, but quick to do what he had no choice but to do. What gathered within the True One put a glow on the face. What he gave did not go beyond the power of his virtue. He could be harsh as any in his world, arrogant and uncontrollable, a hard man, heart gone elsewhere, words forgotten. He took punishment to be the body, ritual to be the wings. He took knowledge as timeliness, and the Power of Virtue as his only force. Taking punishment as the body, he was kind when he had to kill. Taking ritual as wings, he moved freely in his world. Taking knowledge as timeliness, he saw that there were times when he had no choice but to act. Seeing the Power of Virtue as his only power, he was one whose own two feet were sufficient to get to the top of any hill. Yet people persisted in thinking he worked hard to get there.

What he loves is One. What he doesn't love is One. What he takes as One is One. What he doesn't take as One is One. What is at one is the companion of heaven. What is not at one is the companion of humanity. When neither heaven nor humankind is victor or vanquished, we find what is meant by the True Human.

Life and death are fate. They are constant as dawn and dark. This is "heaven." Humankind has those things it cannot have: this is all in the *fact* of things, the way things are. These *things* all have heaven as a progenitor and all embrace it. How much more shall they embrace that which is greater? People accept their princes as their superiors and lay down their lives for them. How much more shall they be willing to die for that which is true?

When the source runs dry and fish are stranded on dry ground, together they will breathe moisture on one another and wet one another with their spit. But how much more would they enjoy forgetting each other in a river or a lake? Rather than praising Yao as a sage or cursing Chieh as a tyrant, it is better to forget them both and enter the flow of the Way.

The Great Clod that loads me down with form and belabors me

with life, eases me with age and releases me in death. If I take life as good, I must therefore take death as equally good.

You may sink your boat in a creek, hiding it as well as a mountain may be hidden in the mist, and call it safe. Then some midnight a strong man comes along and loads it on his back and off it goes. Completely in the dark, some still don't see that although you can hide the small within the large, there may still be things that get lost. But if you hide All-under-heaven within All-under-heaven, there's nothing to get lost. This is the great fact that dawns from the heart of things.

Yet you will dare to try on a human form, already in itself so close to punishment, and still you will seek joy there. But having that form, ten thousand changes will come and go before you even begin to know an end. Can there be a victor here in the quest for that joy?

So the sage of old wandered in a world of things that can never be lost, and dwelt there like an infant. Living long is a good; dying young is a good. Springing from the womb is a good; running out the string in the winter of life is a good. All people take him as a model. How much more so may they take as a model the string that runs through the ten thousand things, that which all and every single change awaits? The Way is of fact and faith. Yet it does not *act*. It has no form. It can be passed on, but it can't be received. It can be gotten, but it can't be seen. It is its own root, its own branch. Before there were heaven and earth, from the beginning within the beginning, solid as an infant, it *was*. It gave spirit to the spirits, spirit to the gods. It is beyond the Great Ultimate Poles, the *T'ai Chi*, and yet not high. Beneath all the Six Directions, it is not deep. It is longer than antiquity itself, yet it is not old. Hsi Wei got it, and drew the line between heaven and earth. Fu Hsi got it, and united with the Breath Mother. The Dipper got it and from the earliest times has turned unerringly. The sun and moon got it and have never rested. K'an P'i got it and united with K'un Lun. Ping Yi got it and explored the Great River. Chien Wu got it and made his dwelling in the Great Mountain. The Yellow Emperor got it and rose into the cloudy heavens. Chuan Hsu got it and dwelt in the Palace of Mysteries. Yu-chiang got it and took his stand at the Northernmost Pole. The Queen Mother of the West got it and made her seat at Shao-kuang. There is no knowing her beginning, nor knowing her end. Peng Tzu got it and lived from the time of Shun to the time of the Five Lords. Fu Yueh got it, and after he was minister to the Warlike Ting, who made All-under-heaven his own, he made the Eastern Anchor Point his chariot, and straddling the Basket and the Tail, took his place among the constellations.

⤳

NAN-P'O TZU-K'UEI SAID TO THE HUNCHBACKED WOMAN Nu Yu, "Your years are many indeed, yet you have the face of a suckling baby. How can this be?"

"I've heard the Way, that's all."

Nan-p'o Tzu-k'uei said, "May I study the Way with you?"

"Oh, no! No way. You're not the man for it. There was Pu-liang Yi," she said. "He had the talent to make a sage, but not the Way. I have the Way of the Sage, but not the talent. I wanted to teach him. You'd think I could have made him bear the fruit of sagehood. But it wasn't so. To deal with the talents of a sage through the Way of the Sage also depends upon changes. But I kept at it, showing by not showing, and after three days in the cocoon of meditation, he was able to put All-under-heaven outside him. Once he could put it all outside himself, I stayed with him, and in seven days he was able to put *things* outside himself. Once he was able to put *things* outside him, I stayed with him, and in nine days he could put *life* outside him. Once he could put life outside him, it dawned on him, and in the light of that dawn, he could see that he was alone. When he saw that he was alone, he knew past and present as nothing, and knowing past and present as nothing, he was able to enter into no-death/no-life, to see that what kills life is not death, that what lives life is not life. As for things, there was no thing he would not escort away, nothing he would not welcome, nothing he would not destroy, nothing he would not bring to completion. This is called Opposing Repose. Opposing Repose means, 'after opposition there is completion.'"

Nan-p'o Tzu-k'uei asked, "Can it be that you are alone in having heard this?"

"I heard it from the disciples of Assistant Ink," she said, "who heard it from the grandchildren of Oral Tradition. Oral Tradition's grandchildren heard it from Wide-Eyed-to-the-Brilliant-Light, who heard it from All-Ears-to-Sounds, who heard it from Needing-to-Use, who heard it from A-Folk-Song, who heard it from Mysterious-Original-Dark, who heard it from Silent Emptiness, who heard it straight from Suspected-It-Already-in-the-Womb!"

Tsu Ssu, Tzu Yu, Tzu Li and Tzu Lai were all walking together when they said, "Whoever can make Nothing his head, life his back, and death his butt, whoever knows death and life, being and being gone, to be one body; I'll be friends with him." The four looked at each other and laughed. Without a doubt in heart or mind, they became fast friends.

Then, suddenly, Tzu Yu fell ill. Tzu Ssu went to inquire after him.

"Isn't it amazing," Tzu Yu cried. "The creator of things is twisting me like this—a crooked hump for a back, my guts on top, my chin hiding out in my navel, my shoulders higher than my head, and my neck bones pointing toward heaven! The *ch'i* of my yin and yang is as messed up as wet feathers!" But with heart and mind unconcerned, he wobbled to the well and peered in. "Oh," he said, "the creator of things is making me all twisted."

Tzu Ssu asked, "Don't you hate it?"

"Perish the thought! How could I hate it? It may well turn my left arm into a rooster. Then I can keep watch in the night. It may well turn my right arm into a crossbow bolt, and then I'll have owl to roast. It may well turn my buttocks into wheels, and then, with my spirit for a horse, I'll never have need for a carriage.

46

"I got my life," Tzu Yu continued, "when the season came. I lose it as it flows away. I'm at peace with the seasons, and dwell in their flow where neither sorrow nor joy can enter. In the old days, they called this 'cutting free from the noose.' If you can't cut yourself free, things will knot you up. But things have never been victorious against heaven. What is there to hate?"

Then Tzu Lai suddenly fell ill, his lungs rasping at the edge of death. His wife and children gathered about him wailing and weeping. Tzu Li, who had come to ask after him, cried, "Shoo! Get out! Don't interrupt the change that is dawning in him." Then he leaned in the doorway and said to Tzu Lai, "Isn't this amazing! Creation! Change! What will it do with you? Where will it go with you? Will it make you a rat's liver or a bug's elbow?"

Tzu Lai replied, "When father and mother tell their son to go east or west or north or south, their wish is his command. Yin and yang are surely no less than parents to a man. They have urged me on toward death. If I refuse to listen, am I not merely one who can't recognize the dawn? What fault of theirs would that be?

"The Great Clod loaded me down with this form," he continued, "and burdened me with life. It eased me with age and will release my own heart and mind in death. Thus, if I make life a good, I must make death a good as well.

"If a master swordsmith were smelting today and the metal leaped up and said, 'I *must* be made into the famous Mo-ye sword,' the smith would take it for metal of bad omen. Now, once I've taken a human form, I may insist, 'A man! A man!' But once I take heaven and earth as a furnace, and creation and change as the Great Smith, what could go on that I could not accept? Having come to this, I'll sleep. Then I shall awaken."

⤳

TZU SANG HU, MENG TZU FAN, AND TZU CHIN CHANG were friends. They said, "Whoever can be together with nontogetherness, do together with noncooperation, whoever can rise up to heaven wandering on the dawn's rising dew, stirring things up no end, together forgetting each other, lost in life with no string to run out . . . " The three looked at one another and laughed, not one heart in disagreement. So they were friends together.

Quietly, an idle moment passed. Then Tzu Sang Hu died. He hadn't been buried when Confucius heard of it and sent Tzu Kung to help with ceremonies. Tzu Kung found one of the friends weaving frames for the molting of the silkworm cocoons while the other played a lute. The two harmonized, singing:

> "Oh, Sang Hu came; oh, Sang Hu came!
> Now he's gone back to being what he truly is,
> While we must go on being human!"

Tzu Kung rushed in, asking, "May I dare to ask how you can be singing in the presence of the corpse?"

The two looked at him. "What does this one know about the meaning of ritual?"

Tzu Kung returned to report to Confucius. "What sort of men are these? They know no discipline at all, putting even the bones of the ceremony aside. They sat beside the corpse and *sang*, with no expression on their faces. I don't know what to call them. What sort of men are these?"

Confucius said, "They ramble outside the boundaries. I ramble within. Within and without—the twain shall never meet. My sending you to offer condolences was crude. They are coeval with that which creates and changes, and they wander the single *ch'i* of heaven and earth. For them, life is a tumor, a growth hanging from them with death as its only excision. They forget their own livers and gall bladders and leave even their eyes and ears behind. They reverse the wintry end and the womb of beginning. They haven't a clue. Blindly, they make their imperial progress beyond the dusty realm, wandering toward the cause of nondoing. Why should they make a show of vulgar ceremony for the eyes and ears of the common herd?"

48

Tzu Kung asked, "Why then, Master, do you remain within these boundaries?"

"I am one," the master said, "whom heaven condemned to go with clipped wings. And you, too."

"Tell me more about boundaries."

"Fish were created together with the waters," Confucius said. "People were created together with the Way. What is at one with water goes deep in a pool and finds all its needs fulfilled. What is at one with the Way, having no duties, lives a settled life. So it is said, 'Fish forget one another in the rivers and lakes; people forget one another in the arts of the Way.'"

"What about people," Tzu Kung wanted to know, "who don't fit within boundaries?"

"Misfits," Confucius said. "Misfits are those who don't fit within humanity's boundaries, but nevertheless fit exactly within heaven's. The small man of heaven is a prince among men. Humanity's princes are the petty men of heaven."

Yen Hui asked, "When the mother of Meng-sun Ts'ai died, he wailed in mourning but without tears. His heart felt no stab of pain, and he conducted her funeral with no apparent grief. Although he failed at all three, he is nevertheless considered a model of true mourning throughout the state of Lu. Can there really be one who can't get any real substance, but can still win a good name?"

"Meng-sun did it all," Confucius said. "He got out ahead of 'knowing.' There are things that he would have simplified, but couldn't, but he simplified quite a bit. Meng-sun doesn't know the why of life nor the why of death. He doesn't know what comes before and what comes after. He's almost changed into a *thing*, and he's just waiting for his not-knowing to change. And as it is *about* to change, how can we know that it *hasn't* changed? Or, if it's not going to change, how can we know whether it hasn't? Is it only you and I who haven't already awakened from this dream? *That* one can have his form trampled without his heart and mind suffering violation. Where dawn lives, death is not a fact. Meng-sun is awakened, and where men are wailing, he too wails. He knows a self that is his own. Must he insist upon joining it to some 'I'? And what 'I' is his 'I' supposed to know? You may dream you are a bird and fly into the heavens. You may dream you are a fish and swim deep within the source. But we can't know whether the speaker is the dreamer or an awakened one. Making do is not as good as laughing. Laughing's not as good as opening up. Just open; let changes happen. There you will find your wings and become one with heaven."

Yi-erh Tzu went to see Hsu Yu, and Hsu Yu asked, "What directions did you get from Yao?"

"Yao told me to practice benevolence and righteousness, and to make clear in my words what is right and what is wrong."

"And still you've come to my little crossroads!" Hsu Yu cried. "Yao's already branded you with 'benevolence and righteousness,' and cut off your nose with 'right and wrong'! How could you still go wandering without direction, following any random path?"

"Although that may be so," Yi-erh Tzu said, "might I not ramble around the edges?"

"Won't work!" Hsu Yu declared. "A blind man can't see the eyes in a beautiful face. The sightless can't tell yellow robes from green."

"Well," Yi-erh Tzu answered, "Wu-chang lost her beauty, Chu-liang lost his strength, and the Yellow Emperor's knowing perished—all in the heat of the furnace and the working of the smith. How can you know that the maker of things will not release me from my brand, put a patch on my nose, and put me up on the chariot of completion to follow *you*, sir?"

"That's a thought," Hsu Yu said. "You never can tell. I'll give you a rough outline: My teacher, ah, my teacher—he minces the ten thousand things real fine, but he doesn't do 'righteousness.' He's a mist anointing ten thousand generations, but he doesn't do 'benevolence.' He's been around longer than antiquity itself, but he doesn't do 'old.' He covers heaven and bears up earth, carves and engraves innumerable herds of forms, but doesn't do 'skill.' This is the way he goes."

⟿

"I'm getting filled with it," Yen Hui said.

"What do you mean?" Confucius asked.

"I've gotten all the way to forgetting benevolence and righteousness."

"Well done. But you're not there yet," Confucius said.

Meeting Confucius again on another day, Yen Hui said, "I've gotten to forgetting all about ritual and music."

"Well done. But you're not there yet."

Yen Hui said, "I'm getting filled with it."

"What do you mean?"

"I'm sitting forgetting."

"What do you mean by 'sitting forgetting'?" Confucius asked, shifting from foot to foot.

"My limbs and trunk fall away," Yen Hui replied, "my intellect is discarded, all form left behind, split from 'knowing' as I find identity in the Great Connection. That's what I mean by 'sitting forgetting.'"

"If you *identify*," Confucius said, "you can be without preferences, ever changing, beyond even constancy. So you have born fruit as a sage. I beg permission to follow behind you."

⟿

Tzu Yu was Tzu Sang's friend. As it had been drizzling constantly for ten days, he said, "I'm afraid Tzu Sang may fall ill," and packed some food to make a meal for him.

When he got to Tzu Sang's door, he heard a sound like singing—or like crying. The voice accompanied the striking of lute strings:

"Oh, Father? Oh, Mother?
Heaven! Oh, humanity!"

There was something unbearable in the voice as it rushed to find its way out of the verse. Tzu Yu entered, saying, "Your song— why is it like this?"

"I was pondering," Tzu Sang said, "what has brought me to this farthest pole, and I can find no answer. How could my father and mother have wished me such poverty? Heaven covers all, without partiality. Earth bears it all. How could heaven and earth serve me alone such poverty? I sought the one who'd done it, but I couldn't find it. And yet I have arrived at this farthest pole. Such is destiny."

Answers for Emperors and Kings

[CHAPTER 7]

NIEH CH'UEH QUESTIONED WANG NI. AFTER ASKING four questions without getting a single response, he jumped up with joy and ran off to tell Master Rush-coat.

"So now you know?" Master Rush-coat asked. "Yu-yu didn't measure up to T'ai. Yu-yu still treasured benevolence and tried to use it to draw men together. He got men, but he never got to the realm of 'not-man.' T'ai slept soundly, and when he awakened went about his business. He could be a horse or a cow. He knew fact and faith. The power of his virtue was near true. He never even entered the realm of 'not-man.'"

CHIEN WU WENT TO VISIT MAD CHIEH YU. CHIEH YU asked, "What was it that Start-in-the-Middle said to you the other day?"

"He told me that the 'princely man' should draw forth his own standards and regulations from within himself. Then none among men would dare not listen and be transformed."

Mad Chieh Yu said, "That one cheats virtue! Ruling All-under-heaven thus would be wading across the ocean, boring a well in a river, or making a mosquito lift and carry a mountain. Does the governance of a sage have anything to do with appearances? He stops, upright, at the One. Only then he goes on; then he can do what needs doing. A bird flies high, beyond the reach of snares and arrows. A rat digs deep beneath the great ceremonial mounds to get beyond the reach of men boring in to smoke it out. Of course, these two small creatures have no knowledge."

~

T'IEN KEN WANDERED ON THE SUNNY YANG SIDE OF YIN Mountain. When he came to the Featherwater River, he ran into a man with No-name, and questioned him, "Please let me inquire about All-under-heaven."

The man with No-name said, "Get away! You crude creature! How can you ask such an ugly question? I am about to be Man, the creator of things. When I'm feeling oppressed, I mount the bird Subtle Confusion, and getting beyond the Six Directions, wander off to the village of Wherever, to dwell in the wilds of Broad Fine Fields. Why must you come running at the mouth with your questions about the ordering of the world to disturb my heart and mind?"

T'ien Ken asked again, and this time No-name answered, "Let your heart and mind ramble in the insipid; harmonize your *ch'i* with the indifferent. Follow *things* as they do what they do, taking no profit. All-under-heaven will be governed!"

~

YANG TZU CHU WENT TO SEE LAO TAN AND SAID, "THERE is a man here, quick as an echo, strong as a roof beam, with enlightened insight into things. He studies the Tao untiringly. Can such a man be compared to an enlightened king?"

Lao Tan replied, "Compared to a sage, this one's a careless mechanic bound to his task, belaboring his form and striking fear into his own heart and mind. It's said that it's the elegant external markings, the decoration, of the leopard and the tiger that attract the hunter. The cleverness of the monkey and the ability of the terrier to catch rats earn them their chains. Do you want to compare one like this to an enlightened king?"

"The enlightened king," Lao Tan continued, "his accomplishments shelter All-under-heaven, and yet he seems selfless. He lets change provide all things, and the people don't worship him. Standing upon the fathomless, he wanders where there is nothing."

⇜

IN THE STATE OF CHENG, THERE WAS A SPIRIT MEDIUM named Chi Hsien who could predict whether people would live or die, exist or perish, find calamity or prosperity, long life or premature death. He could predict the timing of such events to the year, month, week, and day, as if he were himself a spirit. Whenever the people of Cheng saw him, they dropped everything to run away. When Lieh Tzu first saw him, it was as if heart and mind felt drunk in his presence. He rushed home to report to Master Winepot, saying, "I've always believed that your Way was the Way *there*. But now there's one that goes farther."

Master Winepot replied, "I've shown you my outer appearances, but not yet my substance. Have you really mastered my Way? If you have a flock of hens but no cock, will you get fertile eggs? You've shown your Way to the world in order to find followers. That's why this man can read your face. Let him come with you to try me."

On the next bright day, Lieh Tzu brought the shaman to see Master Winepot. When the shaman emerged, he exclaimed to Lieh Tzu, "Woo! Your master's a dead man! There's no life in him. He doesn't have a week. What I see in him is strange indeed. What I see is wet ashes."

His sleeves soaked with his tears, Lieh Tzu entered to report to Master Winepot.

"Just now," Master Winepot said, "I showed him my earthly appearance, hidden and unwavering like the first bright sprouts. He probably thought that the power of my virtue was shutting down. Bring him again."

Bright and early, they returned again. When the shaman emerged from his interview, he said, "What great luck for your master that he ran into me! His illness has taken flight. He's full of life. What I saw before was just the blockage of his energy."

Lieh Tzu entered and reported this to Master Winepot.

"This time," Master Winepot said, "I showed him my Heavenly Field, where neither appearance nor substance enters and the workings come straight from my heels. He most likely saw 'the good' at work. Bring him around again."

When Lieh Tzu brought the medium once again, he emerged saying, "Your master is inconsistent. I can't read anything from his face. Get him to straighten up, and I'll give him a reading."

Lieh Tzu reported this to Master Winepot, who replied, "I've just shown him the Great Unconquerable Liquid Centering. He most likely saw the workings of my *ch'i* coming into balance. Where the water in the wake of a Great Sea Creature makes a whirlpool. Stop up water and it makes a whirlpool; let the water flow and it makes a whirlpool. There are nine kinds of whirlpools. I have three dwelling here in my Great Liquid Center. Bring him again."

At dawn the next day, they returned. The shaman shuffled around, then completely lost it and ran off.

"Follow him now, if you still want to," Master Winepot instructed.

Lieh Tzu followed but couldn't catch up to him. Eventually he returned and reported to Master Winepot, "He's gone. I couldn't catch up and now I've lost him."

"This time," Master Winepot said, "I showed him my ancestral teacher before it began to begin. I showed him emptiness, wriggling like a snake. He didn't know who or what I was as I bowed and wavered, billowed and flowed. So he and his fortune-telling fled."

Lieh Tzu realized he hadn't yet begun to learn anything. He went home, remaining inside for three long years. He did all the chores for his wife and fed the pigs as if they were people. He showed no affection for the affairs of the world, giving up the ostentatious for the plain. He stood alone inside himself like a clod of earth. And amid the flutter of confusion and division, he was at one to the end of his string of days.

DON'T OPEN YOUR DOOR TO FAME. DON'T BECOME A dwelling place for schemes. Don't try to bear up the duties of the world. Know no master. Let your body be the infinite. Follow the path of not-possessing. Be all heaven has given. Don't look for gain. Be empty, that's all. The one who's gotten there uses heart and mind like a mirror, and doesn't go to see things off nor go out to welcome them. Such a one responds, but doesn't treasure, and thus conquers things while remaining uninjured.

THE EMPEROR OF THE SOUTHERN SEA WAS CALLED HURRY Up. The Emperor of the Northern Sea was called Suddenly. The Emperor of the Middle Between was Muddle. Hurry Up and Suddenly often went to the land of Muddle, where he treated them with goodness. Hurry Up and Suddenly wanted to repay his virtue and decided, "People all have seven holes—to see, hear, eat, and breathe with—but Muddle alone has none. Let's see whether we can't help by boring some." Every day they bored him a new one, and on the seventh day, he died.

Webbed Toes

[CHAPTER 8]

WEBBED TOES OR AN EXTRA FINGER POKING OUT—these are natural enough, but they have nothing to do with the Power of Virtue. Warts and tumors may hang from our forms, but they have nothing to do with our nature. There are many who make arts of "benevolence" and "righteousness" and go so far as to claim a place for them among the five vital organs, but this isn't staying straight with the Way and its Power. What webs toes is a useless flap of flesh. Hands with an extra finger sticking out have just sprouted a useless digit. And those who want to claim webbed toes and sprouting fingers as among our vital organs are obscene, depraved, and crude.

In performing "benevolence" and "righteousness," they create a multiplicity of crafty methods of *seeing* and *hearing*. But those whose sight is extra bright are confused by the five colors, made depraved by artful decoration and by the bright blue-greens and yellows of shining brocade garments. Am I wrong? Look at Li Chu.

And those whose hearing is extra keen are confused by the five notes, and made depraved by the six tones and the sounds of metal, stone, silk, and bamboo in the high ceremonial songs "Yellow Bell" and "Ta Lu." Am I wrong? Consider Shih Kuang.

People with an extra finger of "benevolence" pluck at their virtues and finger their nature just to hear the sounds of their own names, making All-under-heaven march to the fife and drum of the method that just doesn't make it. Am I wrong? Look at Tseng Tzu and Shih.

And people with the webbed toes of rhetoric just heap up bricks and knot together rat-tails of argument, rambling among "hard" and "white," "same" and "different," for no more than a moment's reputation. Am I wrong? So much for Yang Chu and Mo Tzu. All these share Ways that are no more than extra fingers and webbed toes. None of them is about to set All-under-heaven straight.

One who wants to set things straight can't lose sight of the facts of nature and destiny. For one like this, what's united is not webbed, what stands apart is not extra, what's long knows no excess, and what's short is not without sufficient footing. The duck's legs are short, but if you stretch them, he'll be anxious. The crane's legs are long, but if you shorten them, he'll be sad. It's just so with nature: the long has nothing to be broken off; the short, nothing to be drawn out. And there is no reason to grieve.

If "benevolence" and "righteousness" are not facts of humanness, how much sadness do "men of benevolence" bring about? Cutting apart webbed toes brings on weeping. Gnaw off that extra finger and there will be howls. Perhaps the webbing leaves you with too few toes, the sprouting with too many fingers, but alteration results in common grief.

In these times, "people of benevolence" stand with glazed eyes gazing out upon the calamity of this world of grief, while those who aren't benevolent bite off the facts of nature and destiny to get wealth and status. Therefore I say, "benevolence" and "right-

59

eousness" are not facts. Yet from the time of the Three Dynasties, what a clamor, oh, what a clamor they've caused!

Those who wait for the curve, the line, the compass and the square to set things straight are paring away at their own nature. Those who use cords to bind and glue to stick things firmly are making inroads into the power of their virtue. Those who bow and scrape to ceremonial ritual and music and prattle on about "benevolence" and "righteousness" in an effort to satisfy the hearts and minds of All-under-heaven lose the constancy of the way things go.

All-under-heaven has a constancy in the way it goes on, and in accord with this constancy, what is curved is not made by means of a craftsman's tool, what's straight doesn't depend on the carpenter's line; the round doesn't need the compass, nor does what's square need squaring. Things that aren't broken don't need gluing. What cleaves together doesn't need binding. In All-under-heaven, all things pass into being, none knowing by what they live and grow. Likewise all things attain what they attain, and there is no knowing how or whence they get it. In this, the ancient past and the present are not two. Nothing's been broken off. Nothing is missing.

So how is it that "benevolence" and "righteousness" go on and on patching and pasting, rambling at *work* within the Way and its Power, making every heart under heaven wonder, "This? Or that?" Small doubts make methods change. Great doubt makes nature change. How do I know? Since the sage Shun grasped "benevolence" and "righteousness" to instruct All-under-heaven, everyone's gone racing off after fame for "benevolence" and "righteousness." Isn't this letting "benevolence" and "righteousness" change their nature? Let me explain. From the time of the Three Dynasties on down, everyone has let *things* change their nature. Mean men risk their bodies for profit. Knights risk theirs for fame. Great ministers risk their bodies for the sake of their families, the sage for All-under-heaven. All these may differ in what they do and in the fame or infamy they gain, but in wounding their nature by risking their bodies, they are one.

An expert shepherd and a little girl both herded sheep. Both lost their flocks. What was the expert doing? He was studying some writing he'd brought along. And the little girl? She was playing. What these two were doing was completely different, but they were equals in losing their sheep.

Po Yi died for fame at the foot of Mount Shou-yang. Robber Chih died for gain on top of the Eastern Height. What the two died for wasn't the same. Their wasted lives and wounded natures were equal. How can we praise Po Yi and blame Robber Chih? Of all those who put their lives at risk in All-under-heaven, if they do it for "benevolence" and "righteousness," the vulgar name them "gentlemen." And if they risk life for wealth, they call them "mean." But what they risk is one. So there's a gentleman and a mean man here, risking their lives and wounding their nature, a Robber Chih and a Po Yi. But how to tell which is the gentle man and which the mean?

Those who train their natures in "benevolence" and "righteousness," although they become the equals of Tseng Tzu and Shih, are no more than that expert shepherd I mentioned before. If they bend their natures to the five flavors, although they become the equals of the Grand Chef Yu Erh, they are not what I call expert. Give over their natures to the Five Notes? Though they equal Shih Kuang, they will not know what I call *hearing*. If they give themselves over to the Five Colors, though they become the equals of Li Chu, they will not learn what I call seeing clearly. What I call expertness isn't what followers of "benevolence" and "righteousness" believe. My expertise lies in the Power of Virtue. That's all. What I call expert isn't what's called being benevolent and righteous. It's bearing up under the facts of nature and destiny.

What I call hearing is not what you do with your ear to the door. It's listening to yourself. What I call seeing clearly doesn't involve seeing anything else, just seeing yourself clearly. One who can't see himself but can only see others can't gain himself, but gains only for others. He gets what others need, oblivious to his own needs. One who is always at the service of others is never his

own, is a slave. And it's in this that Po Yi and Robber Chih are together—the same: obscene, depraved, and crude.

And me? My heart is fearfully short of the Tao and the Power of
Virtue. At best, I wouldn't dare to fall into the grasp of "benevolence" and "righteousness," and at worst, I won't dare to be obscene, depraved, or crude.

Horses' Hooves

[CHAPTER 9]

ORSES' HOOVES CARRY THEM THROUGH FROST AND snow. Their coats protect them from cold winds. They munch grass and drink water. On winged feet they fly over dry land. This is the true nature of the horse. Even if horses had great towers and fine halls, they'd have no use for them.

Then along comes some Po Lo and says, "I'm *good* at ruling horses." He puts fire and knife to them in the name of grooming. He brands and breaks them. He binds and hobbles them with full tack and imprisons them in stalls inside a stable. This alone kills two or three of every ten horses. Then he starves them and leaves them thirsty. He makes them trot and prance and run in line. He teams them side by side. He troubles them with bits and breast-bands and harries them with the crop or the whip. By this time a good half of the rest have died.

The potter cries, "I'm *good* at ruling clay! I can make it round with the compass or square with the square." The carpenter cries,

"I'm *good* at ruling wood. I can make it crooked with the curve-arc or straight with the line." But by nature, how much do the clay and the wood care to be made to match compass or square, curve-arc or line?

Yet generation after generation honors Po Lo, saying, "He was *good* at ruling horses." They honor the potter and the carpenter, saying, "They are *good* at ruling clay and wood." And they make the same error with regard to those who "rule" All-under-heaven. I'll stand here and sing it straight from the heart: those who are *good* at ruling All-under-heaven are not *right*.

People have a constant nature. They weave to clothe themselves, they till to eat. This is called sharing the Power of Virtue, being one without forming classes. This was called Heaven's Mandate, given freely. Thus, a generation that's gotten there, to the Power of Virtue, walks true to the earth and sees true to the lie of the land. They act in concert with the seasons; their mountains know no outlaw's tracks and trails; their marshes know no boats or bridges. The ten thousand things flock and grow, side by side. Birds and beasts flourish in their flocks. Grasses and trees grow tall. You can leash a bird or beast and ramble. You can bend down the branch and peer into the nests of magpie or crow.

So: a generation that's gotten to the Power of Virtue lives as one with birds and beasts and stands side by side, of one clan, with the ten thousand things. What would they know of "gentleman" and "commoner"? They are as one in non-knowledge. The power of their virtue is not separate. They are as one, undesiring. This is called the simplicity of unworked wood. In the simplicity of unworked wood, the nature of the people is achieved.

Then along comes some sage, hobbling cripple-footed after his benevolence and righteousness, and everyone in All-under-heaven begins to know doubt. And by the flourishes of their music, the gesture of their ritual, All-under-heaven begins to be divided. If the unworked simplicity of things were left unshattered, who could make vessels for the sacrifice? If the white jade were left unsmashed, who could make little jade baubles for the court ceremony? If the Tao and its Power were not thrown out, where could benevolence and righteousness find room? If nature and fact had not been separated, what would be the use of music and ritual? If the Five Notes were not cast into chaos, who would need the Six Tones? The destruction of the simplicity of the un-worked merely for the sake of making vessels is the crime of the craftsman. The destruction of the Tao and its Power for the sake of benevolence and righteousness is the error of the sage.

Now horses, living on the land, eat grass and drink water. When happy, they twine their necks and rub together. When angry, they turn their backs to one another and kick. This is what horses know. But add a yoke and a moon-shaped plate on the fore-head, and horses know boundaries and limits, they know they are enslaved. Then, slyly, they look sidelong and arch their necks to bite. They thrash about, trying to expel the bit and shake free of the reins. They have learned now, from their capable hearts, how to be outlaws. This is the crime of Po Lo.

In the time of Ho Hsu, humans lived without "knowing" what they did, and went without "knowing" where. With food in their mouths, they were happy, drumming their bellies as they wan-dered. This was all people were able to do.

Then along came some sage, twisting and bending to rites and music in order to "reform" All-under-heaven's form, and hanging forth the sprouting extra fingers of benevolence and righteous-ness to try to move the hearts and minds of All-under-heaven. It was only then that the people began to prance on tiptoe, addicted to "knowing" and struggling to go home to bed with profit. There was no stopping them. This also is the crime of the sage.

Baggage Gets Stolen

[CHAPTER 10]

I F YOU'RE GOING TO PREPARE FOR THIEVES WHO SLASH baggage, rifle bags, and smash open boxes, you'll use good cord and tight lashing, strong locks and latches. This is what this generation is in the habit of calling "knowing." It may be just so, and yet when a big strong thief gets here, he'll shoulder the boxes, heft the bags and sling the baggage over his back, and run off. His only worry will be that you may not have made your locks and latches fast or lashed your cords tight enough. So. The one who's earned a name for "knowing" has really just been storing goods for the Big Thief.

Let me explain. What the world calls a knowing person is merely one who piles up goods for the Big Thief, right? And what the world calls a sage is just the Big Thief's guard. How do I know? Consider the ancient state of Ch'i. Its neighboring towns were within sight of one another, so close they could hear each other's cocks crow and dogs bark. There were hunting grounds for net and

66

snare, and farmlands for spade and plow filling more than two thousand square *li* within its four borders. The way its ancestral temples and its altars to the soil and grain were established, and the way its towns and villages were ruled—was there even one instance that didn't follow the method of the sage? It was such a place, and yet T'ien Ch'eng-tzu, in the dawn of a single day, murdered the Prince of Ch'i and robbed him of his land. Nor was the domain itself all that he stole. He stole the very methods of sage rule! Thus, although T'ien Ch'eng-tzu gained a name as a thieving bandit, his own body enjoyed the same peace as that of Yao and Shun. The small states didn't dare say that he was not what he should be, and the great states didn't dare bring charges. For generations, his progeny have ruled in Ch'i. Is this not, truly, robbing not only Ch'i, but also stealing the methods of the sage's knowledge? All that to guard the body of a thieving bandit!

I'll try to explain. Among those known by the world today as "one who has arrived at knowing," is there even one of them who isn't just storing up stuff for the Big Thief? Among those who are called "one who has arrived at sageliness," is there even one who isn't just guarding stuff for a Big Thief? How do I know this is true? In ancient times, Lung-feng was beheaded, Pi Kan was disemboweled, Ch'ang Hung was torn asunder, and Tzu-hsu was crushed. Though these four masters were all worthies, they themselves could not avoid getting their wings clipped.

When one of Robber Chih's band asked, "Do thieves have the Tao?" Chih replied, "How could we get along without the Way? There's the wild idea about what might be hidden in a room, and that's 'sageliness' for your thief. Being the first to enter—there's your courage. Being the last to exit—that's righteousness. Knowing whether or not you can pull off a job—*that's* knowing. Dividing the take—*there's* your benevolence. All-under-heaven has never seen a really Big Thief who hasn't mastered these five things."

Now look at it this way—a good person who doesn't get the Tao of a sage can't establish himself, nor can a Chih who doesn't get the Tao of a sage get along without it. In All-under-heaven, the good are few, the not-good are many. So the sage profits All-under-heaven but little, and injures it much. So it is said, "When the lips are gone, the teeth get cold," and, "It was the thin wine of Lu that got Han Tan besieged." Causes may be clear, or they may be obscure. Thus it is that when the sages came to life, great thieves arose. Cudgel the sages, and forget the thieves. Then All-under-heaven will begin to be ruled. Just as when the streams dry up, their beds are empty; and when the hills are leveled, the pools are filled; so when the sages die, big thieves won't arise. With All-under-heaven equal and at peace, there'll be no reason for sages or thieves. But if the sages don't die, big thieves won't stop.

The more weight we give to the rule of the sage, the more we give to the profits of Robber Chih. When we give the people the standard peck and bushel, we teach them to cheat by the peck and the bushel. When we give the people scales and steelyards to weigh with, we teach them to cheat with the scale. When we give them contracts and official seals to bind good faith, we give them contracts and seals to steal with. And when we force them to re-form with benevolence and righteousness, we teach them to steal with benevolence and righteousness.

How do I know? The man who steals a belt buckle gets executed while the man who steals a kingdom becomes a feudal lord. Within the gates of feudal lords, benevolence and righteousness thrive like babies. Is this not simply stolen benevolence and righteousness, and isn't this the whole "knowing" of the sage? So men rush after the Big Thieves, trying to make lords of themselves. They steal benevolence and righteousness, the pecks and bushels and scales, contracts and seals of profit. Carriages and crowns have no power to persuade them, nor can ax and block dissuade them. These merely add weight to the profit of Robber Chih and make him even less dissuadable. This is the error, the excess, of the sage.

It used to be said, "Fish mustn't leave the pool, the state's in-struments of profit must not be shown to the people." Now these "sage" people are mere instruments of profit to the state. They aren't the instruments of the enlightenment of All-under-heaven.

When you cut loose from the sages, you cut off the big thieves. Throw out your jade! Smash your pearls! Then the little thieves won't get started. Burn your contracts and break your seals, and the people will stop haggling. Overthrow the methods produced through the knowledge of the sage, and you'll begin to be able to talk common sense with people again. Mix up the Six Tones. Burn flutes and lutes and plug Blind Kuang's ears, and then they'll begin to really hear again. Destroy decorations, mix the Five Colors, paste Li Chu's eyes tight shut, and in All-under-heaven, they'll begin to see the light again. Destroy the curve-arc and the line, cast out the compass and square, break the fingers of Craftsman Ch'ui, and in All-under-heaven, they will begin to know their own skills again.

So it was said, "The greatest of skills has the appearance of clumsiness." Wipe out all traces of Tseng Tzu and Shih, gag the mouths of Yang Chu and Mo Tzu, throw out benevolence and righteousness, and the power of the virtue of All-under-heaven will be born of dark mystery, equal to heaven again. When people begin to see the light, All-under-heaven will no longer burn. When people begin to hear again, All-under-heaven will no longer be bound. When people know what they know again, All-under-heaven will no longer know doubt. When people begin again to know the Power of Virtue, All-under-heaven will no longer be depraved or crude. Tseng Tzu and Shih, Yang Chu and Mo Tzu, Master Kuang, the Craftsman Ch'ui, and Li Chu—all of them sought the power of their virtues outside themselves, dazzling All-under-heaven into a blind confusion. Their methods were useless.

Do you alone not know of that ancient generation that got to the Power of Virtue—Yung Ch'eng, Po Huang, Li Hsu, Fu Hsi, and the rest? In those days, the people used knotted cords to keep their records. They made good food and beautiful clothing. Joy was just a habit to them. Peace flourished within their ancient doorsills, tranquility beneath their roofs. Although they were within sight of neighboring lands and shared cock-crow and dog-bark, these people grew old and died without ever bothering to go visiting. Such a time you may call well ruled.

But now something makes the people stretch their necks and raise their heels to stand on tiptoe and cry, "Look! There's a worthy man over there!" And they pack up their provisions and hustle off after him. Thus they cast aside their near and dear and lay aside their duty to their host. Their footprints link the borders of feudal lords, their carriage tracks criss-cross a thousand *li*. This is the fault of those above, the result of their addiction to "knowledge." When those above are sincerely addicted to this kind of knowing, they can't know the Tao. Then All-under-heaven knows the Great Chaos.

How do I know this is so? The great *knowing*, the technology of bow and crossbow, net, stringed arrow, and all sorts of ingenious devices, throws the birds into chaos in the skies. The *great knowledge* that lets people make hooks, lures, nets, and weirs, sets fish into chaos in the water. Fences, pitfalls, snares, and cages arise from great knowledge, and they set animals in the wild into chaos. The knowledge that creates deceit and poisonous ambiguity, that fiddles with distinctions about *hard* and *white*, that stirs the dust about sameness and difference—this knowledge is great indeed. It is by this knowledge that doubt is made the habit of the people.

The crime is addiction to knowing. Thus it is that in All-under-heaven they know only to seek after what they do not know. None of them knows to seek after what they already know. They all know to call false anything they think not good, but they don't know to call false what they take to be good. And this is the Great Chaos—it blots out the light of sun and moon from above; below, it burns the vital spirit of hill and stream; between, it skews the succession of the seasons. Crawling bug or fluttering thing, there is none that hasn't lost its true nature, the heart it was born with. That's the power of addiction to technical knowledge—it throws All-under-heaven in chaos. Since the Three Dynasties, it's come down just so. The people who sow and multiply are set aside, while the lackey flatterer is advanced. Simplicity and not-doing are abandoned. What's taken to heart is the song-and-dance that tumbles All-under-heaven.

Staying Home, Possessing Nothing

[CHAPTER 11]

I'VE HEARD OF STAYING HOME AND BEING SELF-POSSESSED in All-under-heaven; I have not heard of "ruling" All-under-heaven. If you stay home, do you need to fear that you will corrupt the heart All-under-heaven possessed at birth? If you possess yourself alone, must you worry that the Power of the Virtue of All-under-heaven will slip away? And if the heart that All-under-heaven was born with is not corrupted and the power of its virtue is not displaced, will All-under-heaven need anyone to possess and rule it?

In ancient times, when Sage Yao ruled, he made All-under-heaven happy. People all took joy in their natural hearts, and their hearts were never quiet. When the tyrant Chieh ruled, he made All-under-heaven sick to death of life, so people felt only the hard lot of the hearts they'd been born with. Those hearts knew no simple satisfaction. To know no peace and know no satisfaction is to be without the Power of Virtue, and who could last long without

71

that power? When the people were too happy, they leaned toward yang. When they were too angry, they leaned toward yin. When both yang and yin were in excess, the seasons fell out of sequence, hot and cold could no longer harmonize, and their disorder wounded human form. People let happiness and anger lead them from their marks and they began to dwell in inconstancy, so that the tigers of anxiety took up residence in their hearts and minds. They couldn't get what they needed. They were always stopped midway and never accomplished their ends. Then, for the first time, there began to be ideas in All-under-heaven that were not simple, actions that were not plain. And so Robber Chih, Tseng Tzu, and Shih came along. Now, even if All-under-heaven were made the reward of the "good," it still wouldn't be enough, and if All-under-heaven were used to punish the evil, it wouldn't be sufficient. Despite the greatness of All-under-heaven, there's not enough of it to provide reward and punishment.

Yet ever since the birth of the Three Dynasties, everyone has been haggling and struggling over nothing more than reward and punishment. What time would they have for the facts of nature and destiny? For these, the enjoyment of sight means debauching themselves in sex; enjoyment of hearing means debauching themselves with music. Enjoying benevolence? Throwing the Power of Virtue into chaos. Enjoying righteousness? Perverting principle. Enjoying ritual? Embracing artifice. Enjoying ceremonial music? Drawing near depravity. Sageliness? Mere magic arts. Enjoying knowledge? Picking nits.

When people are at peace with the facts of nature and destiny, these eight things may exist or may perish. When the people are not at peace with the facts of nature and destiny, these eight things begin to twist and warp the people and bring chaos to All-under-heaven while seeming to be approaching honor and cherishing these things. Such is the state of doubt in All-under-heaven. They don't just commit their excesses and get on with it—they fast before speaking of them; they kneel upon mats and make offerings to them; they drum, dance, and sing hymns before them. And there's nothing I can do.

If a prince can't have what he wants and is stuck instead with holding sway over All-under-heaven, there's nothing better than nonaction. Not-acting, he can be at peace with the facts of his nature and destiny. Since ancient times, one who valued his own body above All-under-heaven could be trusted with All-under-heaven; one who loves his own body more than he loves running All-under-heaven may be given rulership. Thus a prince who can refrain from cutting himself free of his five vital organs, who can keep from teasing apart his seeing from his hearing, will be able to dwell a long time in his corpse with the vision of a dragon, silent as the source, with the voice of thunder. As his spirit moves, heaven and earth will follow. Pliant to nonaction, the ten thousand things will trail behind him like little clouds of steam. And what time shall he have for "ruling"?

⌒⟩

Ts'ui Chu asked Lao Tan, "If you don't *rule* All-under-heaven, how can you perfect the human heart and mind?"

Lao Tan replied, "Don't fuss with heart and mind. It can be pushed down or boosted up, but up or down is a prison, a death sentence for heart and mind. Pliant to the soft and gentle or hard, heart and mind can cut, carve, and polish. Its heat can burn fire; its cold freezes ice. It's so quick that in the space of a nod it can flit twice beyond the four encircling seas and back again. Its dwelling place is the silence of the source. Its motion is the drape of constellations whirling down the sky. It's a racing courser, beyond being bound. No more than this is the human heart and mind.

"In ancient times, the Yellow Emperor was the first to use benevolence and righteousness to fuss with the hearts and minds of humankind. Yao and Shun worked themselves raw to nourish the forms of All-under-heaven. They grieved their vital organs for the sake of benevolence and righteousness, and bore down upon their very blood and *ch'i* to set up laws and standards. Yet there were still those they could not win over. So it was that Yao had to send Huan Tou to Mount Chung, banish the three Miao tribes to

Three Cliffs, and ship off Kung Kung, the minister of public works, to the City of Darkness. This is not what I'd call winning over All-under-heaven.

"Then we get down to the age of the Three Kings, when All-under-heaven lived in terror. At the bottom were your Robber Chihs; at the top, Tseng Tzu and Shih. Then the Confucians and the Mohists arose together. Then even happiness and anger came into doubt. Then ignorance and knowledge competed at cheating. Good and bad called each other false. Truth and falsehood turned to slander, and All-under-heaven withered. The power of great virtue no longer held all things together as One. Nature and destiny went soft and runny and ran off. All-under-heaven was addicted to knowledge, and the people grew distracted. Then came the executioner's ax, the amputator's saw, to bring people to order; then came the rope and the tattoo branding of prisoners to teach about murder; and finally, decisively, the hammers and drills that bored seven holes in Muddle. All-under-heaven was in thorny chaos. The crime lay in fussing with people's hearts and minds. So worthy people slunk off to live beneath great mountain peaks, and lords of ten thousand chariots hid, trembling in their own ancestral shrines.

"The executed dead of this generation lie in a heap. Prison slaves are yoked together in a crowd. And those who suffered amputations gaze upon one another constantly as Confucians and Mohists strut out from among the masses of cuffed, shackled men.

"My heart cries out, 'Can this be so? They know no fear. They will not listen to their hearts. They know no shame.' That's how it is.

"Nor have I yet seen the knowledge of the sage that was not the latch of the yoke, or benevolence and righteousness that were not the clasps of shackles. Thus we come to see that Tseng Tzu and Shih are no more than the first whistling arrows that sound the attack of Tyrant Chieh and Robber Chih.

"So I say: cut down the sage. Reject his kind of knowing, and All-under-heaven will be ruled."

⟜

THE YELLOW EMPEROR STOOD AS SON OF HEAVEN FOR NINEteen years, All-under-heaven turning at his command. Then he heard that Kuang Ch'eng-tzu was up on Mount Empty Togetherness and went to visit him.

"I've heard that you have made it to the true Tao," he said. "May I enquire about its essence? I want to find the essence of possessing heaven and earth, nurturing the five grains, and nourishing the people. I want to learn to manage yin and yang to aid all living things. How am I to do it?"

"All you really want to know about," Kuang Ch'eng-tzu replied, "is the material qualities of things. All you'll manage is their dissolution. Since you came to rule All-under-heaven, the *ch'i* of the clouds falls like rain before it's fully gathered; the leaves of grass and trees fall before they're even yellow; the light of the sun spills out on the waste. You're a slick-tongued seducer. How would that give you footing from which to speak of true Tao?"

The Yellow Emperor withdrew, gave up All-under-heaven, built a special hut, got a white rush mat, and stayed alone for three months. Then he went to see the master once again. When he found him, Kuang Ch'eng-tzu was napping, facing south. The Yellow Emperor crept forward humbly, bowing his head low, and asked, "I have heard that you, my master, have arrived at true Tao. May I dare ask how to rule my body so that it may endure a great long time?"

"Now that's a good question, isn't it?" Kuang Ch'eng-tzu jumped up. "Come. I'll speak to you of the true Tao. The essence of true Tao is the chaste deep secrecy of mysterious darkness. The poles of true Tao are obscured in dark silence. No looking, no listening. Wrap your spirit in silence. Then your form will straighten of its own accord. You must silence your heart and mind to the point of clarity. No belaboring your body. No stirring up your essence. Then you live long indeed. When your eyes see nothing and your ears hear nothing and your heart and mind know nothing, then your spirit will guard your form and your

75

form will live long. Be cautious. Keep your heart true within. Shut your doors on the external. A lot of knowing is a loss. I'll take you up on the Great Brightness and get you to the source of perfect yang; I'll lead you through the Gate of Secret Darkness to the source of perfect yin. Heaven and earth have a manager already. Yin and yang are experts. Guard your own body cautiously, and all things will of themselves grow strong. I guard this unity to live in its harmony. Therefore I have kept up this body for twelve hundred years, and *my* form has not withered."

Bowing low, the Yellow Emperor said, "Kuang Ch'eng-tzu's true title is 'Heaven'!"

"Approach," said Kuang Ch'eng-tzu, "and I'll give you the word. Things can never be exhausted, and yet humankind insists there is an end to the string. There is no measure to things, yet humankind claims they have their poles. Whoever gains my Tao is an emperor above, a king here below. All the doctrines of the hundred schools that prate of illumination are born of dust and will return to dust. But when I leave you, I go to enter the Gate of the Inexhaustible, to wander the wilds beyond all poles. I go to join, and so to constitute, the winged and mysterious brilliant blazing triad—heaven, earth, and humankind. Heaven, earth, and I are constant. Could I face the bonds of dusk? The dusk is far from me. All humanity is bound to die. I alone remain, the glorious master child."

CLOUD GENERAL WANDERED EASTERLY. EMERGING FROM under the Fu-yao tree's branches, he bumped into Big Goose Dummy. Drumming on his tummy, Big Goose Dummy was about to take off like a hopping sparrow. When Cloud General saw him, he hesitated, then stopped, amazed. "Say, Old One," he asked, "who are you and what are you doing?"

Big Goose Dummy kept drumming on his tummy, flapping and hopping like a sparrow. "I'm rambling."

"I have something to ask about," Cloud General said.

"Oh?"

"The *ch'i* of heaven is out of harmony," Cloud General said, "and the *ch'i* of earth is gnarly and knotted. The Six *Ch'i* are out of tune, the Four Seasons out of order. Now I want to harmonize the essence of the Six *Ch'i* for the benefit of all living things. How am I to undertake such a task?"

Still drumming his tummy and scratching his head and sparrow-hopping about, Big Goose Dummy muttered, "I don't know. I don't know."

So Cloud General didn't get his answer.

Three years later, however, when he was wandering east in the wilds where people are even dumber than in Sung, he ran into Big Goose Dummy again. Cloud General was happy, and ran up, shouting, "Oh, Heaven! Have you forgotten me?" He bowed his head to the ground and begged for another audience.

"I wander and ramble without knowing what I seek," Big Goose Dummy said. "A madman, a king dog, I don't know where I'm going. The wanderer, unhaltered, is not deceived by what is seen. What more do you want?"

"I'm quite a mad-dog king myself," Cloud General said. "But the people all follow my trail. I can't get what I want for them, and it is for their sake that I now beg you to speak a single word."

"What throws the warp of heaven into chaos, what rebels against the facts of things?" Big Goose Dummy replied. "What can keep mysterious heaven from accomplishing its ends? What scatters herds of beasts, makes birds cry in the night, and brings bad luck to bugs? I have the idea that it's excess *ruling* humankind!"

"What can I do about that?"

Big Goose Dummy said, "I have an idea: poison. Or take off and fly home."

"Meeting with you," Cloud General said, "is difficult. Let me hear just one word."

"My idea?" Big Goose Dummy said. "Nourish your heart and mind. Stay put and do nothing. Things will change on their own. Drop your form and your body. Drop seeing and hearing. Forget connections. Forget things. Find the Great Unity in the watery vastness. Cut loose from heart and mind. Let go of the spirit. Go forth soulless as a desert. The ten thousand things all return to their roots. They return to their roots without knowing. Get into the pure mud of the Muddle Puddle. Run out your string right there. Never leave. If you're knowing it, you're leaving it. Without asking its name or taking a peek at the facts, things have come down solid from ancient times, all on their own."

"Heaven has handed down to me the Power of Virtue," Cloud General said, "and shown me in dark silence the black dog of mystery. All my life, I've bent and bowed my body in the hunt for it. Now I've captured it." He bowed once more, politely took his leave, and departed.

Iᴛ ɪꜱ ᴛʜᴇ ʜᴀʙɪᴛ ᴏꜰ ᴘᴇᴏᴘʟᴇ ᴏꜰ ᴛʜɪꜱ ɢᴇɴᴇʀᴀᴛɪᴏɴ ᴛᴏ ʟɪᴋᴇ what's like themselves and to despise what is unlike themselves. They desire what's similar to themselves and despise what's different. But at heart, they want to stand out in the crowd. Now whoever has a desire to stand in a crowd at all will never stand out. To rely on the desires of the crowd is not as good as crowding the crowd.

Those who have designs upon the government of a state possessed by another think only of the glories of the Three Kings, and not of how their hearts and minds will become mere targets of calamity. They'd simply trust the kingdoms of humankind to chance. How many chances are there that they won't destroy the kingdom? Not one in ten thousand will survive. And when you destroy a single kingdom, there are more than ten thousand human lives destroyed. How sad that those who would possess a kingdom don't know this!

Possessing territory is a *big thing*. One who possesses a big thing can't just be treated like a thing himself. Because he's not a thing, he can treat things as things. One who clearly sees the way of *thinging* things is not just a thing. How could he rule only the

78

common folk in All-under-heaven? He'd enter and exit the Six Harmonies and wander the Nine Lands. A sole possessor has achieved what we call "getting into the aristocracy."

But the doctrine of the truly great one comes forth like the shadow from the form, the echo returning to the sound. If you are possessed by a question, he will answer. With all that he holds dear, he's the companion of All-under-heaven. He dwells beyond the echo and moves outside direction. He will lead you by the hand beyond the circle of vexations, leading you to wander the realm of causelessness, to come and go without direction, unborn and constant as the sun. When he speaks in hymns of the form and the body, he unites them in the Great Unity. In this Great Unity, there is no self. Without a self, how can you possess possessing? He who fixes his eye on possessing is what we used to call a prince. He who fixes his eye on *nothing* is a friend of heaven and earth.

⤳

THINGS MAY BE LOW AND MEAN, BUT THEY MUST BE BORNE up. People may be rough, but they must be your cause. The business of the state is difficult, but it must not be left undone. Methods may be as hard to find as the tracks of a single beast among the herd, but they must be followed. Righteousness is distant, yet we must dwell there; benevolence is a bias we must make broad. Ritual must be kept full but used sparingly. The Power of Virtue is the center of the target and must be held high. The Tao is One, and not without change. Heaven is of the spirit and must be the source of action.

So the sages watch heaven, but don't try to aid it. They find the power of their virtue but are not bound by it. They go forth with the Tao, but make no plans. They come together with benevolence, but do not set their hearts on it. They're full of righteousness, but they don't treasure it. They accept ritual but not taboo. They conduct the business of the state and don't withdraw from it. They carefully examine methods, but don't let them fall into chaos. They set their hearts on the people and don't take them lightly. So they are *of* things and do not leave them. Things alone are not enough to get things done. There is work that must be done. Whoever doesn't see heaven's brightness will not be pure in the Power of Virtue. Whoever does not follow Tao can't get there from here. Whoever cannot see the brightness of Tao?—Sadly, that heart is false.

What is it I call Tao? There is the Tao of heaven. There is the Tao of humankind. To do not-doing and be honored, that is heaven's Tao. To do doing and thereby get entangled, bound up in things, is humanity's Tao. Heaven's Tao leads the way while the Tao of humankind follows. Heaven's Tao and the Tao of humanity lie far apart. Now *this* is worth looking into.

Heaven and Earth

[FROM CHAPTER 12]

Tzu-kung went south to Ch'u, and, returning by way of the state of Chin, he was passing along the south shore of the Han River when he saw a big fellow working in a one-acre field of vegetables. He was climbing down into a pit well with a pitcher, then climbing out and pouring the water on his crop. It looked like he was working himself to the bone without getting much advantage from his efforts.

"There's a mechanism for this," Tzu-kung said, "and with it, in a single day you could inundate a hundred acres. It doesn't take much effort, and it yields a great advantage. Wouldn't you like to have one?"

The gardener rose up and gave him a look. "How's it work?"

"It's a machine constructed of wood, heavy at one end, light at the other. It lifts the water like a dipper, lots of it, so much that it gushes out as if it were boiling over. It's called a well sweep."

The gardener made an ugly face, then said with a laugh, "I've heard my teacher say, 'Where there are machines, there will be machine problems; where there are machine problems, the mechanical will find entry into the hearts and minds of the people; when people's hearts and minds become mechanical, what's pure and simple is spoiled. Without the pure and simple, the spirit knows no rest. And when the spirit knows no rest, even the Tao can't carry you on.' It's not that I don't *know* about your machine, but that I'd be ashamed to use such a thing."

Autumn Floods

[CHAPTER 17]

WHEN AUTUMN FLOOD SEASON ARRIVED, ALL THE streams poured into the Yellow River, and it grew so broad that from one bank you couldn't tell horse from ox on the other. The River God, delighted with himself, took himself to be the big ram in the herd, the prettiest thing in the world. He wandered eastward with the flowing river until he came to the Northern Sea. Facing east and looking out, he could see no end to those waters.

He nodded and rolled his eyes, and then, looking out over the sea toward *its* god, North Sea Jo, he sighed and said, "The country folk all say, 'Someone who's heard the Tao a hundred times thinks he's better than the common Joe.' They could have been speaking of me. I've heard people slight Confucius's knowledge and make light of the righteousness of Po Yi, without beginning to doubt them. But now that I've laid eyes on your inexhaustible vastness, I realize that if I hadn't come to study at your gate, I'd have been in danger of being the laughingstock of those who are really in the know."

"A frog in a well can't have much to say about the sea," North Sea Jo replied. "It's bound by its own empty space. A summer bug won't have much to say about ice. It's trapped in its tiny time. A cloistered scholar can't have much to say about the Tao, being all wrapped up in his doctrine and dogma. Now that you've seen the great sea, you see where you've come from—you've already begun to talk about Great Principle.

"Of all the waters of All-under-heaven, none is bigger than the sea. The ten thousand streams return to it forever, and yet it is never filled. It boils away at Wei Lu, but the sea has never emptied. It doesn't change with spring and autumn. It knows no drought. It is so much bigger than the flow of the Yellow River that it simply can't be measured. And yet I haven't let this make me take myself for 'big.' I take my form from heaven and earth, and my *ch'i* from yin and yang. Between heaven and earth, I'm like a little rock or a bush on a mountainside. If my mode of being is minor, how could I take myself to be major?

"The place of the Four Seas between heaven and earth is no more than the place of a pile of field stones in the Great Swamp. The place of the Middle Kingdom within the Four Seas is no more than the place of a single seed in a granary. When we speak of all things, we call them 'the ten thousand things,' and humankind is but one of those ten thousand. People crowd the Nine Provinces with their crop-growing, their boats and carts going to and from the marketplace, yet what is the place of humankind but as a single one of the ten thousand things?

"What is it the Five Emperors passed freely down, what the Three Kings struggled over, what people of benevolence grieve over and scholar-knights labor for? No more than this one thing. Po Yi gave it up for fame; Confucius talked about it for the sake of being known as learned. They were just taking themselves for something really big. Wasn't that just like you taking yourself for big water?"

"Okay," the River God answered, "so I'll take heaven and earth for big, and the tip of a hair for little. Okay?"

"Wrong," North Sea Jo answered. "There is no limit to things, no stopping time, no divisions of the constant, and no cause of ends and beginnings. Great Knowing encompasses both the far and the near, neither diminishing the small nor enhancing the large. It examines both present and past, looking deeply without grief, without stretching on tiptoe to grasp what's at hand, because it knows there's no stopping time. It looks deeply into fullness, as into emptiness. Gaining, it knows no happiness; losing, it knows no pain. It knows allotted portions are not constant. The length of a lifetime can't be compared with the length of time before one's birth. Trying to cross the boundaries of the largest thing using the smallest as your vessel, won't you just get so lost that you lose even yourself? Look at it this way—how could you be certain that the tip of one hair was sufficient to measure smallness or that heaven and earth are a measure of what's big?"

The River God answered, "Nowadays the disputers agree that the smallest things are without form and that the biggest can't be contained. Do you believe that?"

"When you look at the big from the viewpoint of the small," North Sea Jo replied, "you can't take it all in. When you look at the small from the viewpoint of the big, you can't make it out at all. The smallest thing is the smallest of the small; the biggest is the biggest of the big. They're different, and it's convenient to note that, but it is also mere circumstance of existence. If things are to be called *fine* or *gross*, they must first have form. Without form, you can't divide things into big and bigger or small and smaller. If you can't contain them, you can't count them. You can talk about the gross and you can think about the fine, but what words can't express and ideas can't delve into—these have nothing to do with either fine or gross.

"So great people don't hurt others. But they don't concern themselves much with benevolence or mercy either. Profit is never *their* motive, but they're not bad tippers. They don't compete for property and wealth, but they don't make a big show of turning it down, either. They don't recruit helpers for their work, but they don't show off their independence. They don't despise the mean and greedy, and while they stay clear of those bad habits, they don't make a display of their difference. They go along with the crowd and don't look down on its glib, fawning leaders. The rank and rewards of the world can't move them. The punishment and blame of the world can't shame them. They know 'right' and 'wrong' are not so easily divisible—no more than 'big' and 'little.' I've heard it said that those with the Tao will not be heard of, that getting the Power of Virtue is not 'getting.' Great people have no selves. They find their parts in life. Now *that's* being there."

The River God asked, "Whether you start outside of things or stay within them, where do you have to get to in order to discern the noble from the mean, big from little?"

"Looking at it from the Tao, there is no noble and no mean. From the point of view of *things*, each takes itself for noble and all others for mean. From the common point of view, noble and mean don't inhere in the individual. They are mere products of opinion. From the point of view of difference, if we take something for big because it's big in some way, then there's not one among the ten thousand things that is not big. If we take something for small because it's small in some way, then there's not a thing among the ten thousand things that is not small. When you know heaven and earth as seeds of grain and grass, when you know that the tip of a hair is a mound or a mountain, then you know something about difference and measurement. As to their *worth*, they have worth according to what they are, and of the ten thousand things that exist, there's not a one that doesn't. Or, if they don't exist, there's not a one that's not worth nothing. Just so, you know that East and West, although mutually opposed, would be nothing without the other being something. That's how shares of worth are settled. When we look at things from the point of view of our own interest, what's right is right, and there's not one of the ten thousand things that is not right; and what's not right is not, and there's not a one of the ten thousand things that's not *not*. When you know how both Sage Yao and Tyrant Chieh each took himself to be right and the other not, then you understand all about picking and choosing.

"Since ancient days," North Sea Jo continued, "Yao gave way to Shun, who ruled in his turn as emperor; but when K'uai yielded to Tzu Chih, Chih perished; T'ang and Wu fought to be kings, and each ruled; Po Kung fought and was destroyed. From this you can see that giving way and fighting are only rituals, the behavior of a Yao or a Chieh, the noble and the mean. Each has its season. None has been constant.

"You can use a beam or a pillar for a battering ram against a city wall, but not to plug a little hole. Which is to say, there are differences in tools. The stallions of Ch'i-chi and Hua-liu could run a thousand *li* in a single day, but they weren't as good at catching rats as a weasel or a cat. Which is to say, there are differences in talents. The horned owl can catch a flea at night and see the tip of a hair, but in dawn's light it is so blinded that it can't tell mountain from grave mound. This is all to say, things have differences by nature.

"So when they say, 'Let's make Right our teacher and do away with Wrong, let's make Rule our master and leave Chaos alone!' they haven't yet lit on the principle that illuminates heaven and earth, nor on the facts of the ten thousand things. This is like saying that heaven's your teacher, but not earth; or yin, but not yang. There is no possibility of such thinking getting anyone into the light, but they keep talking that way nonetheless. They are stupid—or think we are.

"The imperial rulers chose their own successors regardless of family connections. In the Three Dynasties, family lines were the basis of succession. Whoever fell short of the habit of his times was called a usurper. Whoever measured up to such habits was called a rightful successor. Quiet, River God! Be quiet. How would you presume to know at whose gate to study the 'noble' and 'mean,' or in whose school to learn 'big' from 'little'?"

"Then what should I do?" the River God asked. "And what

should I not do? Shall I give up or accept, hold to or push away? How shall I live out my string of days?"

"Viewed from the Tao," North Sea Jo replied, "what's noble and what's mean? They are merely overflow and backwash. Don't leash your knight's heart or you hobble yourself on the high Way. What is much and what little? They're thanks to the patron or alms to beggars. If you go beyond the One, you will fall long and short of the Tao. Be as awful as the prince of the land who doesn't keep the power of his virtue discreet, gentle as the harvest god who never hides abundance. Be as vast as the endless Four Directions that know no bounds. Embrace with your heart each of the ten thousand things. Which deserves more? This is called being unbiased. The ten thousand things are one, and equal. Which is short, which long? The Tao is without beginning and without end, and yet things have their lives and deaths. You can't depend on their becoming. One is empty. One is full. There is no standing in their forms. Passing years can't be held back. Turning seasons can't be stopped. Waxing and waning, filling and emptying, they run out their string and then are born again. This is why, when we speak of True Righteousness, we must first find connection with the principle of the ten thousand things. The life of things is the rush and race of horses, not a motion that is not a change. There is no time that is not movement. What to *do* then? And what to not do? Just be firm about letting things go."

"So what's so noble in the Tao?"

"Who knows the Tao must get to principle. Who gets to principle will stand enlightened about power. Whoever is enlightened about power won't be damaged by things. Those who get to the Power of Virtue can't be burned by fire or drowned in water. Neither cold nor heat can damage them, nor wild beasts injure them. This is not to say that they take these things lightly, but that they can tell *home* from *precipice*. They are at peace with good luck and with ill, and careful where they come or where they go. So there is nothing to harm them. So it is said, 'Heaven's is inside, humankind's is outside.' The Power of Virtue is heaven. Those who know the motions of heaven and of humankind take root in heaven and find themselves in the position to gain the Power of Virtue. There, whether you may dawdle or hurry, bend down or stretch up, you will always return to the *necessary*. That may be called the ultimate."

"What do you mean by Heaven, and what do you mean by Humankind?" the River God wanted to know.

"Horses and oxen have four legs. That's heaven," North Sea Jo replied. "Haltering the horse's head or piercing the ox's nose—that's humankind. So it's said, 'Don't let humankind destroy heaven!' Don't let 'therefores' interfere with fate. Don't let gain lead you astray, toward fame. Be careful! Guard your heart, don't lose it. This is called getting back to the truth."

⌒

THE ONE-FOOTED K'UEI WISHES IT WERE THE MANY-FOOTED Hsien. The Hsien wishes it were a snake. The snake wishes it were the wind, and the wind, the eye. The eye would be as quick as the heart and mind if it could be.

The one-footed K'uei said to the many-footed Hsien, "I hop around on my one foot, and I'm pretty good at it, but you use ten thousand feet. How can you manage that all alone?"

"That's not how it is," the Hsien replied. "Haven't you ever seen anybody spit? *Pittooey!* And out come big drops like pearls and little drops like mist. All different kinds of spittle fly out in uncountable numbers. As for me, I just give a bump to my heavenly mechanism. I don't know how it does what it does. But it does it."

Then the Hsien asked the snake, "I can really go on my many feet, but I can't catch you, even though you're footless. How do you do it?"

"My heavenly mechanism moves me," the snake replied. "How could I change it? What use would I have for a foot?"

Then the snake said to the wind, "I move my spine and ribs to get along—at least there's something there. But now you come whirling up out of the Northern Sea, whirling down to the Southern Sea, and it's like there's not even anything there. How do you do it?"

"Just so," said the wind. "I come whirling up from the Northern Sea and go whirling down to the Southern Sea, and yet if you raise a finger, I'm overwhelmed. The carp that noses its lips above the surface of autumn waters to take a breath of air overwhelms me. And though that's so, I snap great trees and throw down fine halls. I alone can do this! Of my many small defeats, I make a major victory. Such victories, only a sage can win!"

⟿

CONFUCIUS WAS IN K'UANG WHEN TROOPS FROM SUNG encircled him like the folds of a turban, and yet he went on playing his lute and singing.

Tzu-lu, coming in to see him, asked, "Master, how can you be so happy?"

"Come. I'll tell you. I've tried long and hard, " Confucius said, "to keep clear of this extremity, but I couldn't avoid it. It's fate. I've tried for a long time to make my message clear, and gained nothing. The times. In the time of Yao and Shun, there were none who came to this extremity, but not because they knew anything. In the time of Chieh and Chou, no one got his message through, but not for lack of knowing it. The season and the lie of the land make things as they are.

"To cross waters," Confucius continued, "without shying from the sea beast and the dragon—that's the fisherman's courage; to cross the land without shying from the rhinoceros or the tiger— that's the courage of the hunter. With bare blades crossing before him, to look on death as life—that's the courage of the oath-sworn warrior. To know that extremity is fated and that getting through is fated too, to face great hardship without fear—this is the courage of the sage. My fate is settled. There is no mechanism that will save me."

Just then an armored man approached and said, "We took you

for Tiger Yang. That's why we surrounded you. Now we see you ain't him. Please excuse us. We'll be leaving now."

⤳

K<small>UNG-SUN</small> L<small>UNG-TZU</small> <small>SPOKE TO</small> P<small>RINCE</small> M<small>OU OF</small> W<small>EI</small>, "A<small>S A</small> child, I studied the Way of Former Kings and, as I grew up, I was enlightened to benevolent and righteous conduct. I harmonized differences, separated hard and white, the *so* from the *not-so*, the possible from the impossible, came to look down on the 'knowing' of the hundred schools, and silenced the mouths of herds of disputers. I thought I'd gotten there. Now I've heard the words of Chuang Tzu, and I'm lost in them, beyond harmonizing. I don't know whether it's just that I can't rise to his level of argument, or whether I really don't know as much as he does. Now there is nothing that would make me open my beak ever again. I dare inquire about his method."

Prince Mou leaned on his armrest and sighed. He gazed up at the heavens and laughed out loud. "Have you alone never heard of the frog in the caved-in well? He said to the Turtle of the Eastern Sea, 'Oh joy! I can come out and hop around on the railing of the well or go in and rest on cracked tile in the wall. When I go in the water, it comes up to my armpits and holds up my chin. When I wade in the mud, it submerges my feet and covers my shanks. Wigglers and crawdads and tadpoles—none is a match for the likes of me! The whole well's waters are mine, all mine! This is truly being there. Why don't you come in and enjoy the view sometime?'

"The Turtle of the Eastern Sea tried," Prince Mou continued. "But before his left foot was in, his right foot was stuck. As he shuffled to back out, he told the frog about the sea, 'A thousand *li* is not enough measure to span it; a thousand fathoms will not measure its depth. In the time of Yu, when it flooded nine out of ten years, it didn't get any fuller. In the time of King T'ang, when there were seven droughts in eight years, its banks didn't show any sign of shrinking. To be unmoved by any cause, long term or short; to neither advance nor retreat in the face of much or of little—this is the great joy of the Eastern Sea.'

"When the frog heard this, he was properly surprised, and, as if he'd just seen his master coming, he hid. And you—your knowledge doesn't even extend to the boundaries of right and wrong!—and you want to get a view of Chuang Tzu's words. You want a mosquito to shoulder a mountain! You want a horse-worm to gallop across the Yellow River. You're no more equal to this task than that. Your knowledge is not up to discussion of his so-subtle words. And yet you want to take advantage of the moment to gain the advantage of proper study. Aren't you the frog in the crumbling well? But Chuang Tzu? He's just now strolling by Yellow Springs, or leaped up to the deep blue empyrean; or—no North and no South—he's cut free of the Four Directions and floats in the limitless. No East, no West, he is born of the Mysterious Dark and returns to the Great Getting Through.

"And you, despite knowing you've met your master, you want to catch and examine him and tie him up in argument. This is really looking at heaven through a tube or probing earth with an awl. Small. Too small. Go away. Have you never heard of the Shao-ling boys who went to study the Hantan walk? They hadn't yet learned to walk the Hantan way before they'd already forgotten their own way of walking. They had to crawl home on their hands and knees. If you don't escape, you'll forget your old ways and lose your profession."

Kung-sun Lung-tzu's mouth fell open and wouldn't shut. His tongue protruded and wouldn't retract. He gave up and departed.

⌁

CHUANG TZU WAS FISHING FROM THE BANKS OF SLAVE Creek when two ambassadors from the King of Ch'u approached. "Our master wishes to encumber you with the governance of his realm," they said.

Chuang Tzu held his pole and without looking back replied, "I've heard that Ch'u has a Spirit Turtle that's been dead three thousand years; that the king has it wrapped and boxed and stored in the high hall of the ancestral temple. Do you think that turtle would rather have died so his bones could be ennobled, or to be living, dragging his tail in the mud?"

"Why, he'd rather be living, dragging his tail in the mud," the ambassadors agreed.

"Go away," Chuang Tzu said. "I'm dragging my tail in the mud."

⬳

WHEN HUI TZU WAS PRIME MINISTER OF LIANG, CHUANG Tzu went to visit. Someone said to Hui Tzu, "He's coming to succeed you as prime minister." Fearful, Hui Tzu searched for him throughout the kingdom for three days and nights.

When Chuang Tzu finally showed up, he said, "In the south, there's a bird called the Yuan-ch'u. You've heard of it. It takes off from the Southern Sea and flies all the way to the Northern Sea, refusing to rest anywhere except in a Wu-t'ung tree, refusing to eat anything but Lien fruit, and drinking only from sweet springs. Now an owl snags a rotten rat just as the Yuan-ch'u passes over, and he lifts his head and yells, 'Hey! Get away!' Now you've got your kingdom of Liang, you're yelling 'Hey!' at me?"

⬳

CHUANG TZU AND HUI TZU WERE WALKING ALONG THE dike above the Warrior River when Chuang Tzu said, "Note how the minnows dart out to wander where it suits them. This is joy for a fish."

"You're not a fish," Hui Tzu said, "so how do you know what's joy for one?"

"You're not me," Chuang Tzu replied, "so how do you know I *don't* know what's joy for a fish?"

"I'm not you, so I most assuredly don't know what you know.

You're most assuredly not a fish, so my proposition concerning you not knowing what is joy for a fish remains unrefuted."

"Oh, *please*. Let's get back to the root of the issue," Chuang Tzu said. " '*How* do you know what's joy for a fish?' That's what you asked. So you already knew that I knew when you asked me. I know it by walking above the Warrior."

Getting to Joy

[CHAPTER 18]

IN ALL-UNDER-HEAVEN, CAN THERE OR CAN THERE NOT BE perfect joy? Can there even be keeping the body alive, or not?
Nowadays, what's to be done, and what can be depended on; what
is to be avoided, and in what may we abide? What should be approached, and what left behind; what enjoyed and what despised?

What All-under-heaven honors is wealth and noble standing,
long life and a good reputation. What it enjoys is security for the
body, fine flavors, pretty clothing, bright colors, and music. What
it looks down upon is poverty and lowly standing, short life and
bad reputation. What it finds bitter is the body not being well or
safely housed, the mouth not getting fancy flavors, the ear not getting music. If it doesn't get these things, it grows sad, even fearful.
People are concerned only with external form. Isn't this stupid?

So it is that the rich embitter their lives with incessant work,
piling great heaps of things they could never use up. What they
try to do for their forms is all, in fact, external even to their forms.

Those who chase titles of nobility work night into day, the tigers of anxiety always wandering the fields of their hearts and minds. What they do for the sake of their forms puts them very far indeed from their forms. Humankind and grief are born together. The long-lived learn, in the confusion of senility, only to live in cease-less fear of death. How bitter is *that!* How far are they from really doing something for their forms? And the ardent scholar-knight, sworn to offer his life for the sake of others? The world holds him in high repute, but that's not enough to keep his body alive. I'm not sure if the *good* of this "good repute" is really good. If it *is* really good, then "good" is not enough to keep a body alive. But if it's not *really* good, at least it's good enough to keep some others alive.

So it's said, "When loyal counsel goes unheard, step back and do not strive." When Tzu-hsu strove with his ruler, he ended with a mutilated form. True, if he hadn't striven, he'd have had no fame, no good repute. Was his "good repute" really good? Or not?

What people nowadays do in their search for joy—I'm not sure it really bears final fruit in joy. I see the present habit of pursuing joy as the stampeding of a herd, a rushing headlong almost as if in fear of losing their own lives. And yet they call it joy. I'm not sure whether this is joy. Perhaps it is not.

I take nondoing to be real joy. But it is currently a habit to say that it has a bitter flavor. Therefore I say, when you get to joy, there's no joy; when you get to praise, there's no praise. In All-under-heaven, the fruit of right and wrong can't even be agreed upon. Yet although that is so, nondoing can easily settle on what's right and wrong, easily get to joy, and keep a body alive. It's just nondoing that keeps the baby growing.

Let me try to put it into other words. Heaven's nondoing keeps it pure. Earth's nondoing keeps it calm. So the two, in nondoing, harmonize together, and the ten thousand things all change. Vast and imperceptible, they come forth from no place. Imperceptible and vast, they are the perfect image of nonbeing, and the ten thousand things in their variety grow forth from their nondoing.

So it has always been said, "Heaven and earth do nondoing, and no thing is left undone." Oh, humankind! Who can get to doing nondoing?

⟿

CHUANG TZU'S WIFE DIED, AND WHEN HUI TZU CAME TO offer his condolences, he found Chuang Tzu hunkered down, drumming on a pan and singing.

Hui Tzu said, "You lived with this woman, raised children with her, and grew old together. To not weep at her death is enough, already! But this drumming and singing, isn't this a bit too much?"

"No," Chuang Tzu replied. "That's not how it is. When she was first born into death, how could I have not felt grief? But I looked deeply into it and saw that before she was born into life, she was lifeless. Not only was she lifeless, but she was formless. Not only was she formless, she didn't even have any *ch'i*. Somewhere there in the vast imperceptible there was a change, and she had *ch'i*; then the *ch'i* changed, and she had form; the form changed, and she had life. Now there has been another change, and she is dead. This is like the mutual cycling of the Four Seasons. Now she lies resting quietly in the Great Chamber. If I were to go running in 'Boo-hooing' after her, that would certainly show a failure to understand what is fated. So I stopped."

⟿

UNCLE ONE-FOOT AND UNCLE CRIPPLE WENT OUT TO THE Mound of the Dark Lord in the wilds of Kun-lun, where the Yellow Emperor used to take his rest. Suddenly a boil the size of a willow tree popped out on Uncle Cripple's left elbow. He shifted his feet a little and looked at it with apparent disgust.

"Don't you just hate it when it does that?" Uncle One-foot said.

"Perish the thought! What's to hate?" Uncle Cripple replied.

"Life is a loan. The living are borrowers. Life is a junk heap. Death is dawn after this night. You and I came here to ponder change. Change has reached me here. For what should I feel disgust?"

⮌

WHEN CHUANG TZU WAS IN CH'U, HE SAW AN EMPTY SKULL, the bony visage of Sage Yao in form. Tapping it with his riding crop, he asked, "Sir, did you so lust for life that you acted without reason, and so ended thus? Did you lose a kingdom and fall to the headsman's ax, and so end thus? Did you do wrong, and so bring shame upon your father, mother, wife, and children, and so end thus? Did you freeze or starve, and so end thus? Or was it just the turning of your springs and autumns, one after another, that led you to such an end?"

Having spoken, Chuang Tzu took the skull as his pillow and went off to sleep. In the middle of the night, the skull came into his dream and said, "You talk like one of those disputers. I marked your words. You mark mine: of all entanglements of human life that you mentioned, the dead have not a single one. Do you wish to hear me speak of death?"

"Please do!"

"In death," the skull replied, "there is no lord above and no slave below. Nor are there any of the chores and duties of the Four Seasons. The eternity of heaven and earth is our spring and autumn. The joy of the king facing the sunny south upon his throne can't surpass ours."

Chuang Tzu didn't believe it. "If I got the Official in Charge of Fate to bring you back to life," he asked, "to put flesh back on your bones and return you to your father and mother, your wife and children, and all your old friends down home, would you want that?"

The skull furrowed its brow deep as if it were about to suffer the punishment of having one's foot cut off, and replied, "How could I give up the joy of the south-facing king and take up the suffering of humanity again?"

98

⟿

Wʜᴇɴ Yᴇɴ Hᴜɪ ᴡᴇɴᴛ ᴀᴡᴀʏ, ᴇᴀsᴛ ɪɴᴛᴏ Cʜ'ɪ, Cᴏɴғᴜᴄɪᴜs wore a troubled expression. Tzu Kung rose from his mat and came before Confucius and said, "Your disciple dares to ask about Hui's journey east to Ch'i. Why are you looking so sad?"

"It's good of you to ask," Confucius replied. "I very much approve of Kuan Tzu's words of old: 'A little bag can't hold something really big. You can't get water from a deep well with a short rope.' It's true. Fates are appointed, and forms are fitted to their appointed functions. There's nothing that can be added or subtracted. I'm afraid Hui will start talking to the Marquis of Ch'i about the Tao of Yao and Shun and the Yellow Emperor, or even get into Sui Jen and Shen Nung. Then that "lord" will search in himself, and finding nothing even vaguely similar, will begin to feel doubt. When princes doubt, death draws near.

"Haven't you heard about the sea bird that landed long ago beside the city wall of Lu?" Confucius continued. "The Marquis of Lu gave it a ceremonial welcome and offered libations to it in the ancestral temple. He ordered the grand music of the Chiu Shao to be performed for it, and the great sacrifice of an ox, a sheep, and a pig was made as an offering of food. The bird looked mystified and sad. It wouldn't eat a sliver nor drink a single cup. After three days, it died. This was treating a bird like you'd treat yourself, not treating a bird like a bird.

"To treat a bird like a bird, you perch it in a deep grove and let it wander over sandy islets and let it float on rivers and lakes. You feed it eels and minnows and let it fly in a well-ordered flock until it stops. Then you leave it free and easy to choose where it may dwell. Birds despise the simple sound of human voices. How could that sea bird put up with all that racket they put it through? If the grand music of Hsien Ch'ih and the Chiu Shao were performed in the wilds of Lake Tung-t'ing, the birds would fly off, the beasts flee, and the fish dive deep. People, hearing it, would come flocking together to listen and watch. Fish live in water. People die there. They're together inasmuch as they love and hate different things. So they are different. The ancient sages didn't think there was but one kind of talent. They didn't believe all problems were the same. They let the name fit the actuality, and called by the name of *righteousness* only that to which such a name was well suited. This is what was known as 'being prepared to get blessings, and able to hold on to them.'"

Lieh Tzu, picnicking beside the road, saw a hundred-year-old skull. Lifting it from the weeds, he fingered it and said, "Only you and I know not-yet-being-dead and not-yet-being-alive. Are you really grieving? Am I happy?"

The "mechanism" is in all kinds of seeds. Just add water, and they turn into something. At the edge of the water, they might grow into Frog's Robe; sprouted on a slope, they're Slope Plantain; in good soil, that turns into Crow Foot; Crow Foot roots turn into maggots, and the leaves turn into a kind of butterfly that turns into a kind of bug that lives under the stove. It looks like molting snakes and is called *ch'u-t'o*. In a thousand days, the *ch'u-t'o* turns into a bird called Leftover Dry Bones. Leftover Dry Bones' spit turns into a Ssu-mi bug, and the Ssu-mi bug turns into an Eats Vinegar. Yi-loes are born from the Eats Vinegars.

The Yellow Kuang is born from the Chiu-yu bug. The Chiu-yu come from the Mou-jui, which is born from Fleshrot Worms, which come from the Sheep's Groom.

When rams manage to couple with No-sprout Bamboo, Spring Green Tranquility is born. Spring Green Tranquility leads to journeys, and journeys bring horses to life. Horses bring humans to life. Humans eventually turn around and go back to the "mechanism." All things come forth by this mechanism, and all things return to it.

100

Getting to Living

[CHAPTER 19]

ANYONE WHO'S GOTTEN TO THE FACTS OF LIFE WON'T try to make life do what living can't. Anyone who's gotten to the facts of fate won't try to make "knowing" serve where nothing works. To nourish the physical form it is necessary first to have *things*. But there are those who have things to spare who still aren't able to take care of their forms. To have life, it is necessary not to be separated from one's form. Yet there are those who've kept their forms, but still have lost *living*.

When life comes, you can't reject it. You can't stop it when it goes. That's sad, but true. There are those of this world who think nourishing only the form is enough to nurture the perpetual infant that is life, but the fruit of such nurturing is not *living*. What is enough, then? Although they can't do enough, they can't do nothing, either. They can't avoid doing something.

For those who would reject *doing* for the sake of form alone, there's nothing better than rejecting the world. Reject it, and be

101

unbound. Unbound, you may be upright and at peace. Upright and at peace, you will be more alive and the more alive you will remain.

How is it that it's enough to merely abandon the affairs of the world and to take life itself as a sufficient heritage? Abandon the affairs of the world, and your form will be unbound. Let life be enough, and its essence will be undiminished. When your form is whole and your essence eternally beginning again at the beginning, you are one with heaven. Heaven and earth are father and mother of all things; their coming together creates the body; their separation gives it birth. When form and essence remain unnamed, this is what we call being able to move on. With essence beyond essence, you become like heaven.

MASTER LIEH TZU INQUIRED OF THE GUARD OF THE PASS, Kuan Yin, "People who've 'gotten there' can go underwater without getting stuck there. They can walk through fires without getting hot. They can rise high above the ten thousand things without fear. What I'd like to ask is, how do they get to that point?"

"They do it by guarding their pure *ch'i*," Kuan Yin replied. "It's not the sort of thing you can learn, like a skill, nor is it the result of daring. Stay a moment, and I'll explain.

"Whatever has an appearance or a semblance, whatever makes a sound or has a color—they're all *things*. One thing can't be much different from another. Which should take precedence? They're all just bright appearances.

"But what creates things is formless and stays at the still point of the changeless. Now, whoever gets hold of this and dwells in it alone may not be detained, may not be stopped by things. People like this can inhabit a place where there is no excess, can hide in a space that has no hint of a boundary, and can ramble free and easy from the endings to the beginnings of the ten thousand things. They will be at one with the heart they were born with, nourish their *ch'i*, harmonize the power of their virtue, and *get through* to that which creates things. What is heaven-born they sustain, complete, within them. What is of the spirit is never rejected. How could mere things confound them?

"So it is when a drunken man falls from his chariot—though he might be injured, he won't be killed. His bones are put together like everyone else's, but his injury is different. His spirit was whole: he didn't know he was riding; he didn't know he'd fallen out. Fear of death had no way to penetrate his breast. And so he confronted things without a flutter of fear. If one may find a wholeness in wine like this, how much more wholeness may one draw from heaven? The sage resides in heaven; there is no thing there that can harm him. Such a one, though bent on revenge, doesn't wreak it on the weapon of his enemy any more than even the most ill-tempered of men, being struck by a falling tile, would blame the tile. Such a one will bring equality to All-under-heaven, and do away with sentences of death or maiming. So goes the Tao.

"Don't start with the heaven one can know, but with heaven's heaven. Begin with this heaven, and the Power of Virtue comes to life. Begin with the heaven invented by people, and the thieving begins. Don't oppress heaven nor despise humankind, and the people will come to know what's true."

⤿

CONFUCIUS, EMERGING FROM A GROVE IN CH'U, SAW A hunchback snapping up cicadas with the tip of a rod, as easily as if he were picking berries. "An artist!" Confucius cried. "Is there a Tao to this?"

"I have Tao," the hunchback replied. "For five or six months, I balanced two clay pellets on the tip of the stick, and they never fell off. By then, only the tiniest cicadas got away. When I could balance three pellets at a time, I lost only about one in ten. Then I practiced with five pellets, and never dropped a one. Then it was just like picking berries. My body, as it stands, is no more than a dead tree trunk, my reaching arm no more than one of its branches. Though heaven and earth are great and the ten thousand things be many, all I know is cicada wings. How could it come to pass that I shouldn't get them?"

Confucius turned back to his followers and said, "'Use the knight's heart, undivided. There the spirit will congeal.' That old saying certainly applies to this hunchbacked gentleman."

Then Yen Hui said to Confucius, "When I was crossing the rough, dangerous waters at Ch'ang-shen, the ferryman handled the boat like a spirit. So I asked him, 'Can one learn to handle a boat like this?' And he replied, 'It can be done. Many good swimmers have the ability. And then there are your divers. They can do it before they've ever even seen a boat.' I asked him for more, but he wouldn't say. Dare I ask you to explain?"

Confucius answered, "That many good swimmers can do it is because they've forgotten water. As for divers being able to master boating before ever seeing a boat, well, they look at the rough and dangerous depths as you would look on a highland cart track. An overturned boat is no more to them than a stuck cart is to you. Stuck or tipped over, when it's something you've seen ten thousand times before, it's not something that really gets to you. So you can go on without fear.

"Shooting for chips," Confucius continued, "a man might show great skill with the bow; for a brass buckle, he'll try to keep it simple, and take aim. Start him shooting for good yellow gold, and he might as well be blind. His skill remains the same, but as his attention turns toward the prize, externals intrude. When externals intrude, what's internal can get twisted."

When T'ien K'ai-chih had an audience with Duke Wei of Chou, the duke said, "I hear that Chu Hsien has made a study of living. You've been in the swim with him. What have you heard?"

"I've hardly done more than grasp the broom to sweep his courtyard. What could I have learned from the master?"

"Don't be so humble," Duke Wei prodded. "I'm listening."

K'ai-chih said, "I've heard the master say, 'Being good at living is just like being a good shepherd—keep your eye out for stragglers, and whip them back into the herd.'"

"What does that mean?" Duke Wei asked.

"In Lu," K'ai-chih said, "there was Shan Pao, who lived under an overhang in the mountains and consumed only water. He had no intercourse with ordinary folks. At seventy, he had the complexion of an infant. Unfortunately, a hungry tiger found him and devoured him.

"Then there was Chang Yi. There wasn't a mansion or low hut where there was a party he'd pass up. At forty, he was struck by a raging fever and died.

"Shan Pao cared only for internal things, and a tiger ate his outsides. Chang Yi cared only for external things, and a raging fever took his insides. Of these two masters, you could properly say, 'He didn't whip up his stragglers.'

"Confucius said, 'Hiding what's inside like some treasure, trying to show off like the shining sun, or making yourself stand right in the middle, on both legs, solid as a tree, here-and-now? The third of these courses will doubtless lead you to get a reputation for going to extremes.'

"Now, when people are setting out across dangerous country where it's said one in ten may be waylaid, fathers and sons, older and younger brothers will take sword and halberd in hand, and will have a full party of armed followers before they set out. Isn't this wisdom, indeed? But what people ought to also acknowledge as dangerous are things like lying on their mats, eating or drinking. For these, people fail to arm themselves with knowledge. *There's* a mistake."

⌒

THE OFFICER OF THE ANCESTRAL SACRIFICE, DRESSED IN the black square-cut hat and robes of his office, went up to the pig sty and said to the pigs, "Why should you fear death? I'll feed you luxuriously for three months, fast you fastidiously for ten days, and finally hold the strictest of vigils over you for three days, after which I'll lay out mats of white rushes and set out your shoulders and hams on the carved stand of the sacrifice. That will do very nicely for you, won't it?"

Now, if you were working for the pigs, you might say, "That's not as good as eating chaff and bran and staying alive here in the sty." Calculating for yourself, you might think, "If I can have noble status in life and be decorated at my funeral, that will do very nicely for me, won't it?" What you would pass up for a pig, you might grasp for yourself. Exactly how is it that you differ from a pig?

⤻

DUKE HUAN WAS RIDING TO THE HUNT BESIDE THE MARSHES with Kuan Chung as his charioteer when he saw a ghost. He grasped Kuan Chung's hand and cried, "Father Chung! What do you see?"

"Your servant sees nothing."

The duke returned to his palace, blathering wildly all the way. He fell ill and remained in his chambers for several days.

Among the scholar-knights of Ch'i, there was a certain Huang-tzu the Bold Speaker. He said, "Sir, you are wounding yourself. What power has a ghost to injure a duke? When one's store of *ch'i* is exhausted, dispersed and not recovered, then there's not enough to let you do anything. If it rises and doesn't fall, then you get real good at being angry. If it goes down and doesn't come back up, you get real good at forgetting things. When it doesn't go up or down and gets right into your center, it controls your heart and mind, and then you're sick."

"But are there such things as ghosts?" Duke Huan inquired.

"There are. The *Li* lives on the hearth. The stove has its *Chi*. The heap of clutter inside the gate is where the *Lei-t'ing* dwells. Down in the northeast corner, the *Pei-a* and the *Kuei-lung* jump around, and in the northwest, the *Yi-yang* makes its home.

In water, you'll find *Kang-siangs*; on hills, *Hsins*; in the mountains, the *K'uei*; in wilderness, the *P'ang-huang*; and in marshes, *Wei-t'os*."

The duke asked, "What does a *Wei-t'o* look like?"

"It's about as big around as a chariot wheel hub," Huang-tzu said, "and about as tall as a chariot shaft. It wears purple robes and a red hat. It hates to hear the thunder of chariots. When it does, it claps its hands over its ears and rears up. Whoever sees one is destined to become Overlord."

Delighted, Duke Huan grinned and said, "That's what I saw!" He straightened his robes and hat and sat up on the mat beside Huang-tzu. Before the day was done, without his even knowing it, his illness was gone.

CHI HSING-TZU WAS TRAINING A FIGHTING COCK FOR THE king. After ten days, the king asked whether it was ready. "Not yet," Chi Hsing-tzu said. "He's still arrogant and set on his own *ch'i*."

After another ten days, the question came again.

"Not yet. He still responds to sounds and sights."

Another ten days passed and the question came again.

"Not yet. He still has a fierce look and an overflow of *ch'i*."

Ten more days brought the question yet again.

"He's almost there. Even when another cock crows, he remains unchanged. Watching him, you'd think he was made of wood. When the power of his virtue is complete, no opponent will dare confront him. They'll all run away."

CONFUCIUS WAS VIEWING LU-LIANG FALLS, WHERE THE water cascades down nearly three hundred feet into billowing rapids nearly forty *li* long. Not even fish, turtles, or other water creatures could swim there, so when he saw a man swimming, he immediately assumed it was an attempt to end a bitter life. He sent his disciples downstream to try to rescue him, but before they'd gone more than a few hundred paces, the man emerged from the flow, hair streaming behind him, singing as he swam up to the bank.

Confucius caught up to him and inquired, "I took you for a sprite. But now I see that you're a man. May I ask, is there Tao to how you go along in the water?"

"Lost," he said, "I possess no Tao. I was born to it. It grew to be my nature, and now it's my destiny. I enter into the whirl and exit from the swirl. I follow the Tao of water, doing nothing of my own. This is how I go along in water."

"What do you mean," Confucius asked, "when you say, 'I was born to it, it grew to be my nature, and now it's my destiny'?"

"I was born on land and raised to know the security of the land. That's how I was born to it. I grew up in the water and learned to know that feeling of security in water, so that's my nature. I don't know how I can do what I do, yet I can. It's my destiny."

~~

THE CRAFTSMAN CH'ING CARVED WOOD INTO BELL STANDS. When he was done, the people who saw his work were startled, as if they'd seen a ghost or spirit.

The Marquis of Lu saw one and asked, "What magical art did you use to make this?"

"Your servant is a craftsman," Ch'ing replied. "What art could I have? But although that is so, I *do* unify around it. When I'm going to make a bell stand, I don't let it gnaw at my *ch'i*. I fast to clarify my heart and mind. When I've fasted for three days, I no longer dare to think of congratulations or rewards. When I've fasted for five days, I no longer dare to think of honors or condemnation, of skill or clumsiness. After seven days of fasting, I've forgotten that I have four limbs and a bodily form. In that moment there is no lord and no court. My craft is all there is. There's nothing to distract me. Then I go into the mountain grove and look upon heavenly nature . . . the perfect form comes, and then I see the bell stand, and only then put my hand to it. If it doesn't come, it doesn't. I just match nature to nature. That's why people suspect the presence of a spirit."

TUNG-YE CHI SHOWED OFF HIS SKILLS AS A CHARIOTEER for Duke Chuang. In advancing and retreating, his line ran straight as a carpenter's. Turning left or right, his curves were as smooth as if drawn with a compass. The duke thought him even better than the legendary Tsao Fu, and commanded that when he completed a hundred circuits of the course, he should come to the palace.

Yen Ho saw Tung-ye Chi making his rounds and went in for an audience. "Chi's horses are going to break down," he declared.

The duke kept his own counsel and did not reply. Presently, however, Chi returned, his horses having indeed broken down.

The duke turned to Yen Ho. "How did you know?"

"The horses were exhausted, and still he commanded them to go on. That's why I said they'd break down."

THE CRAFTSMAN CH'UI COULD DRAW A LINE STRAIGHT AS taut string and make a circle as perfect as a compass because he let his hand change with the change of *things* and didn't let his heart and mind get distracted. Therefore he kept his spirit's abode unified, yet unfettered.

If the shoe fits, you forget your feet. If the belt of office fits, you forget your waist. Knowing may forget right and wrong if heart and mind fit. If you can't be changed by what's internal or made to follow what's external, then you're fit to the task. Begin with what fits and never let it not fit, then you can forget about fitting.

Sun Hsiu called at the gate of Master Pien Ch'ing-tzu. "When I lived in the village," he said, "no one ever said I wasn't a hard-working farmer; in wartime, no one ever said I wasn't brave. Yet when I worked in the fields, I never met with a really good harvest, and when I served my prince, I never gained advancement. Now I'm looked down upon in my village, and I'm sent away by the district officers. What have I done to deserve this? How have I come to face such a destiny?"

"Have you never heard of how the ones who've 'gotten there' go on?" Master Pien asked. "They forget they have a liver and gall bladder. They leave behind their eyes and ears. Wandering on as if lost in a wilderness beyond the dust of this world, they ramble on without duties to perform. This is what is known as 'doing without taking credit, nurturing to maturity, but not possessing.' Now you—you wear your knowledge like a hair ornament to impress the ignorant, and you cultivate yourself so as to appear enlightened before the mean . . . flashing as if you were going around with the sun and the moon in your hands.

"You're still whole," he continued. "Your form's complete, with all the requisite nine holes. You've made your way along without encountering deafness, blindness, lameness, or deformity. Compared to the great run of humans, you're lucky. Where do you get off complaining about your fate? Get out of here!"

Sun Hsiu departed, and Master Pien went inside. After sitting a while, he looked up toward the heavens and sighed.

His disciples asked, "Why does our teacher sigh?"

Pien replied, "Just now Hsiu came, and I told him about the Power of Virtue of one who's gotten there. Now I'm afraid I may have driven him off in confusion."

"That can't be so! Was Sun Hsiu right? Was what the master said wrong? Wrong certainly can't confuse right. And if what he said was wrong, and what our master said was right, then he was confused already, and you're still faultless."

"Not so," Master Pien said. "In antiquity there was that bird who alighted beyond the city wall of Lu. The Prince of Lu wanted to entertain it, and so made a great sacrifice to be offered to it, and had the Chiu Shao music performed before it, intending to bring it joy. But the bird grew sad, blank-eyed, and refused food or drink. This is what's called treating a bird like you'd treat yourself. If you want to treat a bird like a bird, perch it in a grove or float it on a river or lake, and let it eat snakes, if it pleases. Give it a secure place, and there it will find sufficiency.

"This Hsiu is a man of honest speech but little experience. And now I've gone and spoken to him of the Power of Virtue of the ones who have really gotten there. It's like giving a mouse a chariot ride or playing sacred bells and drums to a quail in the wilds. How could he *not* be startled?"

The Mountain Tree

[CHAPTER 20]

CHUANG TZU WAS TRAVELING IN THE MOUNTAINS WHEN he saw a huge tree with luxuriant limbs and leaves in abundance. When a lumberjack studied it, then chose to spare it, Chuang Tzu asked why.

"There's no good material in it."

"This tree," Chuang Tzu replied, "because it has no value as material for anything, will live out its full string of days."

Coming out of the mountains, the master stopped by the hut of an old friend. Delighted, the friend instructed a servant to kill and cook a goose.

"One goose can cackle," the servant asked, "and one can't. Which shall I kill?"

"Kill the one that can't," the host replied.

The next day, Chuang Tzu's disciples asked, "That mountain tree yesterday got to run out its destined string of years because it was of no use. Then the host's goose was cooked because of its lack of usefulness. Where, Teacher, do you stand on this?"

112

Chuang Tzu laughed. "Will I stick somewhere between usefulness and uselessness? Somewhere between seems like the right answer, but it's not—because *there*, you can't keep from being drawn in. But that's not the case if you just get to the chariot of the Tao and the power of its virtue. Then you'll drift or ramble where there is neither praise nor blame. Be a dragon. Be a worm. Change with the season. No need to specialize in anything. You may rise or go down, making harmony your measure. You can drift or ramble with the ancestor of the ten thousand things, a thing *among* things, not treating things as *mere* things. What would there be then to draw you in? Moving like water— this is the method of Shen Nung and the Yellow Emperor. It doesn't work to get wound up in treating things like *things* outside yourself, or to labor at handing down codes of human behavior. If you go that way, joining together leads only to coming apart, completion only to destruction, worthiness to conniving, and unworthiness to being duped. What, after all, is worth getting, what thing would you let pierce your heart? What is there to hold to? It's sad, but if it's not yet in your hearts, my young knights, put *this* there—only the little village home that is the Tao and the power of its virtue."

WHEN I-LIAO OF SHIH-NAN HAD AN AUDIENCE WITH THE Marquis of Lu, he noticed that the marquis looked unhappy. "My prince looks so unhappy. What troubles you?"

"I've studied the Tao of former kings," he answered, "and I have cultivated the way of former princes. I've shown respect to ancestral spirits and honored the worthy. I follow them as if they were my own parents and never live apart from them. And still, I can't seem to avoid calamity. And that's why I am so unhappy."

"The arts you practice to avoid calamity are shallow," Master Shih-nan replied. "The furred fox and the spotted leopard perch in groves on the mountain or crouch in caves in the cliffs. They stay quiet, going about by night, remaining at home in daylight. Even

113

when they're hungry and thirsty, they stay stealthy, sneaking out only along hidden paths beside rivers and lakes to hunt for their food. Yet no matter how set against it they may be, they can't escape the calamity that is the net or the trap. And what's at fault? It's their fine pelts that make for their disaster.

"And is this not true today," he continued, "isn't the state of Lu my prince's pelt? I want my prince to skin his form, to wash all desire from his heart, and to go wandering in the wilderness where there are no people. In the south of Yueh, there is a city called the Kingdom of Sturdy Virtue. Its people are ignorant and simple, short on selfishness, and lacking desire. They know about making stuff, but not about hoarding; about giving, but not about receiving. They can't tell where 'righteousness' fits. They don't know what rituals they ought to carry out. Like madmen and wild women they go about, treading the Great Path. Births make them happy. They bury their dead. I want you to leave this country, break free of its customs. Get on the road that leads *there*, and go on."

"That way is long and dangerous," the marquis said. "There are mountains and rivers. I haven't a cart or a boat."

"If you stop dwelling in haughtiness," Master Shih-nan said, "and leave all conventional dwelling behind, that alone will serve quite well for conveyance."

"But there are no people in that dark forest. Who would be my neighbor? Where would I go for provisions? How shall I eat? How could I ever *get there*?"

"If you cut down on your expenses," Master Shih-nan replied, "cut down on your desires, then even no provisions will be sufficient. On foot, you can ford rivers, you can drift out to sea until you can gaze off forever without seeing the shore. Go forward, go on and you'll never know an ending. Those who come to see you off may leave the shore and hurry home. You will have gone a long way indeed.'"

Shih-nan continued, "One who owns people is bound; one who is owned by people, miserable. So it was that Sage Yao would not own men, nor would he be owned. I want only that you be unbound, freed from unhappiness, so you may wander with the Tao to the Great Emptiness.

"If you're crossing the river in an outrigger and an empty boat rams your craft, even if you're a hot-blooded man, you won't be enraged. But if there's someone in the other boat, you'll yell at him to get out of your way. If he doesn't hear you, you'll yell again. And if he still pays no heed, you'll yell a third time, and follow that with *really* ugly sounds. You weren't angry the first time, but you are now. It *was* empty. Now it's full. If you empty yourself before you go rambling in the world, who will harm you?"

CONFUCIUS WAS SURROUNDED ON THE BORDER OF CH'EN and Ts'ai, and for seven days had no firewood for cooking. T'ai-kung Jen went to console him. "You almost died, eh?"

"It's so."

"You hate death, don't you?"

"It's so," Confucius repeated.

"Let me try telling you how to keep from dying," Jen said. "In the Eastern Sea, there's a bird called the Lazybird. It's not much of a bird. It's always ruffled and molting, and apparently has no abilities. They must help one another in order even to fly, and when they perch, they are propped one against another. None dares go to the front of the flock when it moves ahead, or to straggle when it moves away. When feeding, none goes first. They all prefer the leavings. Because none is cut from the flock, no one can get at them to do them harm. Thus they stay clear of calamity.

"As they say," he continued, " 'the straight tree's cut first, the sweet well the first to be drained.' Your intention has been to wear your knowledge like a hair ornament to startle the ignorant and to cultivate yourself so as to appear enlightened before ordinary folks. You shine and flash as if you were carrying the sun and moon in your hands. So you can't stay clear.

"Long ago, I heard an accomplished one say, 'The braggart has no merit. When merit is accomplished, it begins to decay; when fame is accomplished, it's already on the wane.' Who can put merit and fame away and get back in the great flock of people? For such a one, the Tao flows. It doesn't stay put in bright light. He gets where he's going and doesn't try to make fame a dwelling place. Simple and constant, almost crazy, he brushes over his footprints and sweeps aside his influence. He doesn't *do* merit and fame. Therefore, he doesn't blame others and others don't blame him. You never hear about one who's really gotten there. Why do you want to be famous?"

"Isn't that good!" Confucius exclaimed. He then took leave of his traveling companions, sent off his disciples, and went to the Great Swamp, where he wore skins and bound his hair in cloth and lived on acorns and chestnuts. When he wandered among the animals, their herds didn't flee, and when he went among birds, their flocks didn't fly. If neither bird nor beast despised him, could people?

⌇

CONFUCIUS ASKED OF MASTER SANG-HU, "I'VE BEEN DRIVEN from Lu twice now. In Sung, they cut a tree down on me. I had to cover my trail when I left Wei. I've been in abject poverty in Shang and in Chou. I was surrounded on the border of Ch'en and Ts'ai. Since I've suffered these various calamities, I don't seem to be as well connected as I was. My friends and disciples are scattering. What's the matter?"

"Are you the only one left," Master Sang-hu asked, "who hasn't heard of Lin Hui? When he fled on the collapse of the city-state of Chia, he cast down his jade seal of office—worth a thousand gold coins—and carried away his baby on his back. Somebody said, 'As far as value is concerned, a baby's not worth even a bolt of cloth. And *bother*—a baby is a lot more bother. You threw away your jade seal and carried off your baby. Why?' Lin Hui answered, "The seal and I were united only for profit, while this had to do with heaven. Things brought together for the sake of profit, when they meet poverty, misfortune, calamity, or the threat of bodily harm, will cast each other off. Things that belong together because of 'heaven,' meeting poverty, misfortune, calamity, or threat of bodily harm, will cling even more closely together. To cast off and to cling together are far apart indeed."

"A gentleman's friendship," Master Sang-hu continued, "is like cool water; a petty man's friendship is like sweet wine. A gentleman's conversation leads to strong affection while a petty man's sweetness becomes cloying and grows divisive. Those who come together for no good reason will part for the same."

"I respectfully accept your instruction," Confucius said, and with a light and lively step and easy manner departed for home. He gave up his studies and gave away his books. His disciples no longer came to bow before him, but their affection for him increased.

On another day, Master Sang-hu said, "When Shun was about to die, he charged Yu, saying, 'Use caution. As for the form, let it follow along. As for feelings, let them go where they are led. What follows is not left behind, and what goes where it's led is not belabored. If you're neither left behind nor belabored, you won't depend on cultivation to support your form, and when you don't depend on cultivation to support your form, you certainly won't depend on *things*.'"

~

CHUANG TZU PATCHED HIS OLD COAT WITH PIECES FROM A bolt of rough cloth, lashed on his sandals with hemp rope, and went off to see the King of Wei.

"The old master is in great distress, eh?" the king asked.

"Poor, but not in distress," Chuang Tzu replied. "If one has the Tao and the power of its virtue and yet does not practice it, that one, you could say, was in distress. When your clothes are threadbare and your shoes worn out, that's just being poor, not being used up. It's merely what I call 'not having yet met the proper season.' Is the king the only one who's never seen a monkey climbing high? When he's in a great cedar or catalpa or a camphor tree, he'll swing from limb to limb, master of all he surveys, and not even a renowned archer like Yi or P'eng Meng could get a clear shot at him. But if all he can get into is a bramble bush or a prickly mulberry, he'll go as carefully as a man on a cliff, glancing from side to side and quivering with fear. It's not that his muscle and bone have gone stiff with anxiety—simply that the lie of the land's unsuitable to him. He can't gain sufficient footing to show what he can do.

"Now, if a man lived where those above him dwelt in confusion and were ministered to by disorderly traitors—even if he wanted *not* to appear in distress, how could he hope to? Eh? That was the way Pi Kan got his heart cut out."

WHEN CONFUCIUS WAS REDUCED TO UTTER POVERTY on the border between Ch'en and Ts'ai, seven days without even wood for cooking, he leaned with his left hand on a decaying tree, tapped time with his right on a dead limb, and sang "The Lord of Piao." The instrument could not be tuned and the voice didn't reach any of the prescribed classic modes, but the sound of the wood and the voice of the man, like the sound of a plough turning earth, went straight to the hearts of his disciples.

Yen Hui, arms folded across his chest, turned and studied him. Confucius worried that Hui might admire him excessively and thereby do injury to himself. "Hui," he said, "it is easy to avoid being injured by heaven. It is difficult to avoid being benefited by humankind. There is no beginning without an end. Humankind and heaven are one. Who is it, now, who's been playing?"

"I dare to ask," Hui said, "what you mean by 'It's easy to avoid being injured by heaven.'"

"Hunger, thirst, cold and heat, dwelling in poverty and having your way blocked—these are heaven and earth doing what they do. Just things moving with the flow. They are what we mean when we say, 'Everything passes.' A minister of state doesn't abandon his lord. How much more true shall this be of those who are servants of heaven?"

118

Hui then asked, "What do you mean by, 'It's hard not to be benefited by humankind'?"

"When you are first employed, everything comes to you. Rank and wealth come along together as if they were inexhaustible. This is the harvest of *things*, but it's not something to do with the *self*. The true destiny of a person is beyond this sort of thing. A gentleman is not a bandit. A worthy man is not a sneak thief. If I want *things*, what am *I*?"

Confucius continued, "So it is said, 'There's no bird wiser than the swallow.' Its eye won't alight twice on a spot it finds less than fitting. Even if it drops the fruit it's eating there, it will just let go and get away. It fears people, but it makes its dwelling among them, finding security in eaves and food at their altars to the soil and grain."

Hui asked, "What do you mean by, 'There's no beginning that is without an end'?"

"The ten thousand things change," Confucius said, "but we do not know what brings about that change. How shall we know their endings? How shall we know where they are born? Just stay straight and wait for them. That's all."

"But what do you mean by 'Humankind and Heaven are one'?"

Confucius answered, "There is humankind because there is heaven. There is heaven because there is heaven. That humans can't possess heaven is simply our nature. The sage calmly lets his body go on embodying change and so runs out his string. That's all."

CHUANG TZU WAS RAMBLING AROUND THE LORD'S PARK AT Tiaoling when he saw one weird-looking jaybird coming up from the south. Its wings spanned seven feet, and its eyes spanned a hand. It blundered into Chuang Tzu, brushing his brow before perching in a chestnut grove.

"What sort of bird is this? Its wings are huge, but its movement ungainly; its eyes are very big, but it can barely see!" Chuang Tzu cried. He hiked up his robe and stepped out, cocking his crossbow and steadying his aim.

Just then he noticed a cicada that had found an attractive shady spot in which to forget itself. Close by, a mantis raised its pincers to take the cicada. Concentrating on its aim, the mantis forgot its own form. The weird jaybird observed, aiming to take advantage itself, but in turn losing sight of its own true condition. "Aiiee!" Chuang Tzu cried. "Things are so bound together! Different kinds of creatures all bound together in *this*."

He'd just put away his crossbow and turned to leave when one of the lord's foresters came running up and began to berate him.

When Chuang Tzu got home, for three long months he refused to come into the courtyard to speak with his students. Lin Chu came to him and asked, "Why is it that you have given up holding audience for us in the courtyard?"

"For the sake of my form, I almost lost myself," Chuang Tzu replied. "Peering into muddy water, I took it for a clear pool. I've heard Lao Tzu say, 'When you go where common men go, do as they do.' Just now I was wandering at Tiao-ling and forgot myself. When the weird jaybird brushed my forehead, I wandered into the chestnut grove, forgetting these truths. The forester of the chestnut grove took me for a poacher and might well have clipped *my* wings. That's why I'm not teaching."

⟿

WHEN YANG CHU WAS TRAVELING IN SUNG, HE SPENT THE night at an inn. The innkeeper had two concubines, one beautiful, the other ugly. The ugly one was his favorite; the beauty was out of favor. Yang Chu asked why, and a servant replied, "The beautiful one knows all about her beauty, but we don't see it. The ugly one accepts her ugliness, and we don't see anything ugly about her."

"Disciples, take note!" Yang Chu declared. "Be worthy, but put the thought of worthiness aside. Where could you go and not be loved?"

120

Knowing Wandered North

KNOWING WANDERED NORTH ALONG THE MYSTERIOUS Dark-water and climbed the knoll at Hidden Heights, where he ran into Do-nothing Say-nothing, and said, "There are a few things I'd like to ask you. What sort of thinking and what sort of worrying about things in your mind does it take before you *know* Tao? In what place, in what guise, may I find peace in the Tao? By following what path will I *get* it?"

Do-nothing Say-nothing did not reply to these three questions. He did not just not answer, he didn't know.

Not getting any answers, Knowing returned south of the flashy Whitewater and climbed the Peak of No Doubt. There he saw Mad Mouther, and so asked him his questions.

"Oh! I know!" Mad Mouther cried. "But whenever I start to say it, I forget what I'm about to say!"

Getting no answers there, Knowing went back to the Imperial Palace and got an audience with the Yellow Emperor, and asked him.

121

"Don't think at all!" the Yellow Emperor answered. "Don't worry about any idea. Then you'll begin *knowing* the Tao. In no place, in no guise, will you be at peace in the Tao. When you follow nothing and know nothing, you'll start getting the Tao."

"You and I know this—that one, and the other one, didn't," Knowing said. "Which is right and which wrong?"

"That Do-nothing Say-nothing is right on! Mad Mouther seems right. You and I aren't even close," the Yellow Emperor said. "Those who know don't speak. Those who speak don't know. That's why the ancient sages taught wordlessly. You can't *get* Tao. You can't *get* the Power of Virtue. Benevolence can be endured, but righteousness is a mistake, and ritual is mutual deception. That's why it's said, 'When the Tao is lost, the Power of Virtue is worshipped; when the Power of Virtue is lost, benevolence comes; after benevolence, there's only righteousness; and when that's gone, ritual, the falling flower of the Tao—the face of chaos.' And it's also said, 'Doing Tao, you lose something every day. Loss by loss, you get to doing nothing. And then *nothing* is left undone.' Once we've become *things*, how could it be anything but difficult to get all the way home to the root? Easy, perhaps, for one who is great.

"Life is a follower of death," he continued. "Death gives birth to life. Who knows where the thread of self begins? Human life is gathered *ch'i*. Gather *ch'i*, and that's life. Disperse it, and that's death. Life and death are disciples. They follow one another. Can I call either a calamity? The ten thousand things are one in this, then: what's big and pretty is called wonderful, what's ugly is called rotten. But rotten things change into wonders, and wonders rot in time. So it is said, 'Get through to this: All-underheaven is one *ch'i*.' Therefore, the sage threads all things like shells on a single string."

Knowing asked the Yellow Emperor, "When I asked Do-nothing Say-nothing, he didn't answer. He didn't just not answer, he didn't even know about answering. And when I asked Mad Mouther, he got into telling me but couldn't finish. It wasn't that he didn't tell me. He was in the midst of telling me when he just forgot. But when I asked you, you knew the answer. How can you say, 'We're not even close'?"

"The one who doesn't know is right," the Yellow Emperor replied. "The one who forgot is pretty close. You and I aren't even close *because* we know."

When Mad Mouther heard about this, he said, "That Yellow Emperor is one who really knows about words!"

⤶

HEAVEN AND EARTH POSSESS GREATNESS AND BEAUTY AND use no words. The Four Seasons possess the Brilliant Method but don't discuss it. The ten thousand things possess the perfect principles but do not speak. The sage begins to get from the beauty of heaven and earth the principle of the ten thousand things. This is why the one who's *gotten there* doesn't act, and the sage *makes* nothing. They watch for what heaven and earth have to say.

⤶

NIEH CH'UEH ASKED FOR INSTRUCTION IN THE TAO FROM P'i-i. "If you'll just straighten your form and concentrate your gaze," P'i-i said, "you'll get to heavenly harmony. If you'll just put a hold on your knowing and concentrate on one good guess, the spirit will come to live with you. The Power of Virtue will beautify you. You will come to inhabit the Tao, and you'll just look on, blank-eyed as a new calf. Nor will you be looking for a reason."

But before he was through speaking, Nieh Ch'ueh had fallen asleep. P'i-i was delighted, and went off singing,

> "A form like a rotten stump
> and a heart like ashes,
> Truth is the fruit of his knowing,
> and he doesn't care why.

Dark as the matchmaker,
   in the dark as her mother—
No mind! There's no match for him!
   Who *is* this guy?"

      ↜

SHUN ASKED CH'ENG, "CAN YOU GET THE TAO AND POS-
sess it?"

"You don't even possess your own body," Ch'eng laughed.
"How could you get possession of the Tao?"

"If I don't possess my own body, who does?"

"It's a form heaven and earth has lent you. Life is not your possession. It's a harmony heaven and earth has lent you. You don't
possess the heart you were born with, or your destiny. They are a
course heaven and earth have lent you to follow. Your children
and your grandchildren are not your possessions. They are molted
insect skins, lent you by heaven and earth. So: go on. Without
knowing where. Or stay without knowing why. Eat with no
thought of flavor. The *ch'i* of the yang in heaven and earth is
strong, but even *it* can't 'get' and 'possess'."

      ↜

CONFUCIUS ASKED LAO TZU, "SINCE YOU'RE SITTING HERE
at peace in the sunshine within your own gates this day, may I
ask you about getting to the Tao?"

"Fast. Sit vigils. Perform ablutions and lustrations. Wash heart
and mind in the snow and beat down your 'knowing.' Now, the
Tao—it's cavernous. Blinding. It is hard to find words for it, but I
will try to give you words for its banks and its boundaries.

"The bright was born of darkness; the constant from the formless; the seed of the spirit from the Tao. Form was born of this
seed, and the ten thousand things from this form. Things with
nine holes are born from wombs. Things with eight are born from
eggs. Both come without leaving footprints, and when they go, go

beyond all banks and boundaries. With no gate and no chamber, theirs are the Four Quarters, all bright their domain. Whoever invites their companionship will be strong of limb, straight-forward and far-seeing in thought and deliberation, clear in sight and hearing. Their hearts and minds won't be belabored. They will respond to things without calculation. Heaven can't help but be high. Earth can't help but be broad, sun and moon have no choice but to go on. The ten thousand things can't help but lead people like these. That's what Tao *is*.

"The most learned may not know this, the logician may not find its sweet solution. And so the sage breaks with learning and logic. What can be poured into without ever overflowing? What can be drawn from without ever emptying? That is what the sage holds to. Deep, deep is the source, so like the sea. And lofty like mountains. When its string is run out, it is born to begin again. It moves all the ten thousand things along, never failing. That Way of the Gentleman of yours is a long way from this. What the ten thousand things keep coming to for help—and never leave wanting—that is what the Tao is.

"Here in the realm of the Middle Kingdom, there are *humans*—neither all yin nor all yang—dwelling in their place *between* heaven and earth. Because they are human, they will return to the original ancestor. Far from where they begin, you'll see the sound of life's meaning as an infant's sobbing, 'Wa-wa,' or happily chortling, 'Yi-yi.' And if some live long while others die young, how great, really, is the difference? With only a moment to enjoy, how could there be time to decide whether Yao or Chieh was right or wrong?

"Fruits and creeping melon vines each follow their own rule," Lao Tzu continued. "The ways of human groups also, although difficult to perceive, can be made out. Sages meet with them; they don't oppose them. They pass beyond. They don't preserve them. To harmonize in responding—that is the Power of Virtue. To respond in the instant of first meeting—that is Tao. That's how emperors rise up, how kings get started. Human life between heaven and earth is like the white pony seen through a crack in the wall, a sudden flash to flag the heart, and then gone. In a flood of water from the labor of birth, there isn't one that is not so born. Ebbing and flowing away, there is not a one that does not melt back into earth. A change, and you live. A change, and you die. Every living thing grieves at this. Humankind says no to it and mourns with ritual. But it's just the bow case of heaven being untied, heaven's book bag being dumped clean. Dust? Some trifle? It's the souls moving on, and now the body follows after, and now the great going home. The form that comes to the formless, the formlessness that comes of form—all know these the same. It's not something those who've gotten there take on as a duty. Masses of people turn it this way and that with their words, but those who get there stop all that talk. Those who are still talking aren't there yet. Clever words are not as good as silence. The Tao can't be heard. To plug your ears is better than to listen. This is what's called, 'The Great Getting.' "

TUNG-KUO TZU ASKED CHUANG TZU, "WHERE IS IT THAT you find what you call Tao?"

"There's nowhere it isn't."

"I can't accept that unless you can get more specific."

"In ants."

"Lower than that?"

"In weeds in fields."

"Even lower?"

"In shards and tiles."

"And even lower?"

"Piss and shit," Chuang Tzu said. When Tung-kuo Tzu didn't know how to respond, Chuang Tzu continued, "The problem is that your question isn't really to the point. It sounds like the market master's questions for the pig inspector—making him poke lower and lower down the pig on the theory that the lower you get, the more you can tell about how well fattened the pig really is. You can't insist on 'can't be' or 'has to be.' You'll never get free of things that way. Getting to Tao that way, other big words would work just as well. *Cycles* or *Everywhere* or *United*—all three are just different words for the same reality. What they point to is the One.

"Let's try wandering together to the palace of not possessing anything. We can talk about sameness and coming together no end. Let's do nothing together. We'll be calm and quiet, empty as a desert, clear as water, in tune—and *free*. Spreading our wings will be our hearts' only desire—heading nowhere, not knowing where we'll end, going and coming without knowing where we finally set our heels. We've already been there and back, but we still don't know the end of the string. The two of us, going where we please, emperors of the unbounded vastness. The Great Knowing will come too. There's no knowing it to fail.

"What makes things finds no boundary between itself and things. If things have borders, they are the borders made by words. The border of the unbordered is no border at all. We may speak of filling and emptying, of flourishing and declining, but what makes full and empty doesn't empty or fill. What makes things flourish and decline doesn't flourish or decline. What makes root and branch doesn't root or branch. What causes things to accumulate and disperse does not accumulate and does not disperse."

⤚꜀

Bright-Flash-of-Tailfeathers-in-the-Sun asked Nonexistence, "Do you, sir, possess existence, or do you not?"

Nonexistence didn't respond. And when Bright-Flash studied the face of Nonexistence, there was only a blinding, cavernous emptiness. He spent all day looking, but still didn't see. He listened, but didn't hear. He groped, but could not grasp it.

"There!" Bright-Flash cried. "Who could get to this? Even I can get to possessing nothing, but I can't get to not possessing nonpossession. *He's* gotten to doing non-nothing. Who can follow this?"

JAN CH'IU ASKED CONFUCIUS, "CAN WE KNOW WHAT WAS before heaven and earth?"

"We can!" Confucius said. "The past is still present."

Jan Ch'iu, not knowing how to respond, withdrew. The next day he returned and said, "Yesterday I asked about knowing what was before heaven and earth, and you answered, 'We can. The past is still present.' Yesterday it was clear to me, but today I'm in the dark again. May I ask what you meant?"

"It was clear yesterday," Confucius said, "because your spirit received it first. You're in the dark today because you sought it outside your spirit. No past. No present. No beginning and no end. Children and grandchildren without children and grandchildren? How's that?"

When Jan Ch'iu didn't respond, Confucius continued, "That's it! No response. Not letting life give birth to death. Not letting death put life to death. Do life and death both have something they depend on? Are they One in some body? Is what's born before heaven a thing? What makes things of things is no thing. A thing did not put forth the first thing. Yet there are things. And it's no thing they're in. The sage's love for humankind is a love of no thing. *That* comes of *this*."

Snail Kingdoms

[FROM CHAPTER 25]

K ING YING OF WEI MADE A TREATY WITH LORD T'IEN Mou of the state of Ch'i. When Lord T'ien Mou turned his back on the treaty, King Ying was enraged. He was at the point of sending an assassin to Ch'i when his minister of war, hearing about the plan, came rushing in, red-faced from ear to ear with shame, and said, "You are a Lord of Ten Thousand Chariots, and yet you charge a mere commoner with carrying out your revenge. I beg to be granted twenty thousand armored men to attack him for you. I'll savage his people, capture his cattle and horses, and put the heat to him until he breaks out in boils on his back. Then I'll ravage his capital and when his General Chi flees, I'll beat his back and snap his spine!"

Hearing this speech, Chi Tzu came rushing in, also blushing with shame, and said, "We've been building a city wall with this treaty. It's seven-tenths done. If we knock it down now, those who've labored to build the peace will be bitter indeed. It's been seven years since you have raised an army. *This* is the foundation of your kingdom's wall. The minister of war is an instrument of chaos. You mustn't listen to him."

When Hua Tzu heard them, he reviled them both, saying, "The one who makes such a good case for attacking Ch'i is an agent of chaos. The one who makes such a good case for not attacking Ch'i is also an agent of chaos."

"So what shall I do?" the king asked.

"My Lord must seek the Tao, that's all."

When Hui Tzu heard this, he invited Tai Chin-jen in to audience. Tai Chin-jen said, "There's a creature called a snail. Has my Lord heard of it?"

"I have," said the king.

"There is a country on the snail's left horn called Gore, and on the right horn there is one called Crush. From time to time, they get together to make war on each other for the sake of territory, propping up a few tens of thousands of corpses on some battlefield, and chasing down and wiping out each other's remnant forces for a week or so before returning home."

"Nonsense!" cried the king. "Why this empty talk?"

"May it please your majesty to allow me to fill you in. Do you believe there is a limit to space, the Four Directions, and up and down?"

"There is none."

"Well, then, you know that when your heart and mind have been rambling in the limitless, when at last you return to these lands that can be reached by transport, you find it hard to believe that *these* lands really exist at all. Isn't that so?"

"That is so."

"Among the lands that can be reached by ordinary transport there is a kingdom of yours called Wei. In the kingdom of Wei, there is the city of Liang, and in the city of Liang, there is a king. But is that king distinguishable from the King of Gore?"

"There is no way to distinguish us," the king replied, and when Tai Chin-jen came out, the king sat unsteadily, heart and mind suspended between having and losing.

Tai having come out, Hui Tzu entered for an audience.

"That is a great man," the king said. "Not even a sage has the standing to face him!"

"Blow on a flute, and you'll get a fine high note," Hui Tzu said. "Blow on your sword hilt, and you get the sound of your breath. People swear by Yao and Shun, but talk about Yao and Shun before Tai Chin-jen, and your own breath is all you'll ever hear."

External Things

Y OU CAN'T ALLOW EXTERNAL THINGS TO PENETRATE your heart. That's what got Lung-feng executed, what got Pi Kan a death sentence, what drove Prince Chi mad, what got E Lai killed, and what dethroned both Chieh and Chou.

There is no lord who does not want his officers' hearts to be centered on loyalty. But a loyal heart may be mistaken, and so penetrated to its center. Just so, Wu Yun got thrown in the Yangtze, and Ch'ang Hung died in Ssuchuan, though Ch'ang Hung was so pure that when his body had lain in the earth for three years, his blood was transmuted to green jade.

There are no parents who do not desire filiality from their children, but filial behavior doesn't guarantee the child's heart won't be pierced for want of parental care. So it was that Hsiao-chi went loveless, and even Tseng Shen's heart never knew fulfillment.

Rub wood against wood, you get fire—that's simply so. If metal stays too long by the fire, it will flow. When yin and yang go wrong, heaven and earth are riven, thunder rumbles, and there is fire in the water, fire to burn even the great spirit tree. When human beings are caught between the poles of injury and gain, with nowhere else to run, they may remain as if in a cocoon, unable to complete their transformations, their hearts hanging suspended between heaven and earth, anxious and sorrowful. When profit and loss rub together, a very great heat indeed is the product. It is a fire that will consume great masses of humankind. Not even the constant stillness of the moon that is the heart and mind can overcome these flames, and people standing close by *things* they value may see even the Tao burn away.

⌐

WHEN CHUANG TZU'S FAMILY WAS DOWN TO ITS LAST worn penny, he went to borrow some grain from the Marquis of Chienho.

"Right!" the marquis declared. "I'm about to bring in the tax grain. When I get it, I'll send you grain worth a hundred in gold, okay?"

With the anger in his heart showing clearly in the color of his face, Chuang Tzu replied, "When I was on my way here yesterday, I heard a shout coming from the middle of the road, and when I looked back toward the sound, I saw there was a perch in a puddle in a chariot rut. I said, 'A perch! What are you doing here?' And the perch replied, 'I'm Minister of Waves in the Eastern Sea. If you can get me a dipper or even a cup of water, that would be a real life saver.' I said, 'Right. I'm just on my way south to visit the kings of Wu and Yueh. I'll redirect the West River so it comes this way. Okay?' The anger in the perch's heart showed clearly in the color of his face as he replied, 'I'm out of my element. There's no place for me here. If I can get a dipper or cup of water to wet my tongue, I might survive. But if all I get is this kind of *talk*, the next time you see me it will be in a dried fish shop.'"

⌐

133

KUNG-TZU JEN BAITED A HUGE FISH HOOK WITH FIFTY bullocks, hunkered down on Mount K'uai-chi, and tossed his line out into the Eastern Sea. Day after day at dawn he fished there, and for a full year caught nothing. But in the end, a big fish took the bait and, dragging down the huge hook, headed for the bottom. Surprised, it came up and broke water, leaping, trying to shake the hook. Whitecaps rose like mountains, the waters of the sea were churned into froth, and there was a noise like ghosts and demons wailing, scaring off everything within a thousand *li*.

Once Kung-tzu Jen got hold of the fish, he cut it up and dried it, and from the Chih River east and Ts'ang-wu north, there wasn't anybody who didn't fill up on it. Since then even the most mediocre of storytellers amaze one another retelling this tale.

Now, if he'd shouldered his pole and rushed off to the nearest ditch to angle for minnows and perch, it would have been impossible to land the big one. Those who tie little theories together as lures for landing county offices will also go a long way without getting very far. If you haven't even heard about how Kung-tzu Jen was accustomed to doing things, you are a long way from being ready to lay down lines for the world.

⟳

A GANG OF THOSE CONFUCIAN WEAKLINGS WAS RIFLING A tomb, digging away with the wooden slips that made up the pages of their *Classic of Rituals* and their *Shih Ching*, their classic *Book of Songs*. The big boss weakling called down to them in verse:

"Dawn is breaking;
How's the takings?"

The little weaklings answered, "We haven't yet got the funeral robes free of him yet, but there's a pearl in his mouth, and as it says in the *Book of Songs*,

'Green, green the grain
That grows upon the grave mound;
Living, he gave nothing;
Dead, why should his mouth hold a pearl?' "

Then they grasped his sideburns, pulled down on his beard, and, prying open his jaw by poking his chin with a metal rod, got the pearl free without injuring it.

⌒

A DISCIPLE OF LAO LAI-TZU WAS OUT GATHERING FIREWOOD when he ran into Confucius. He returned and reported to his master, saying, "There's a man out there, long bodied and short legged, slightly hunchbacked, with his ears set way back on his head. He's peering around at everything like he's in charge of all within the Four Seas. I don't know whose family he belongs to."

"It's Confucius! Call him to come in," Lao Lai-tzu cried. When Confucius got there, he continued, "Put away that officious look and that all-knowing expression of yours, and you might become a real gentleman."

Confucius bowed, stepped back, then, shuffling his feet and re-composing his face, asked, "Might I thus advance my affairs?"

"You can't endure the wounds of your own times," Lao Lai-tzu said, "but you're oblivious to your own running rampant over the next ten thousand generations. Are you so crude on purpose, or have you just lost the capacity to recognize consequences? You run rampant in a quest for men's favor. Your whole life is a *shame*. This is the behavior, the 'advancement' of mediocre men drawn together by mean secrets, joined in praise of Yao, in blame of Chieh. Better to forget them both. Better to do away with praise. What goes *against* things is always wounded. Every thing that moves goes wrong. The sages shuffle their feet and wait, embarrassed, at the beginning of things—so that *all* may take part and gain merit in accomplishment. But everything *you* undertake is arrogance and affectation."

135

IN THE MIDDLE OF THE NIGHT, LORD YUAN OF SUNG dreamed that a man with long flowing hair peeped in at the side door of his chamber and said, "I come from where Tsai-lu Stream rises swelling from the earth. I was on embassy from the clear Yangtze to the Lord of the Yellow River. A fisherman named Yu Chu has caught me."

When Lord Yuan awoke, he had his man interpret the dream.

"It's a spirit turtle," the diviner said.

"Is there a fisherman called Yu Chu?"

"There is," his courtiers replied.

"Bring Yu Chu to court."

The next day, Yu Chu appeared at court. "What have you caught, fisherman?" the lord demanded.

"I got a white turtle in my net. It's five feet around."

"Present the turtle to me," the lord ordered.

When the turtle was brought in, the lord wanted to kill it. And he also wanted to let it live. Since he was in doubt, he divined, and the answer came, "Kill the turtle and use its shell in divination. That is auspicious."

So the turtle got shelled, and indeed in seventy-two consultations of the shell by boring and heating, not a single one gave a false prognostication.

Confucius said, "The spirit turtle was able to get audience in the dream of Lord Yuan but was unable to avoid Yu Chu's net. Its shell knew enough to answer appropriately to seventy-two divinations, but not enough to avoid the calamity of being disemboweled. So, knowledge has its problems, and even the spirit has its limitations. Even perfect knowledge may fail in the face of ten thousand schemes. Fish don't know enough to fear a net, though they flee a pelican. But chase out small knowledge, and great knowledge will illuminate you. Get rid of *goodness* and *good* is who you'll be. Every infant learns to speak without a gifted teacher; it dwells with people who can speak."

❧

Hui Tzu said to Chuang Tzu, "Your talk is useless."

"Only when you know what's useless can you start to talk about what's useful," Chuang Tzu replied. "The earth is broad and great, but all that a person needs of it is a place to put two feet. But if you were to dig out everything that those two feet weren't on, all the way down to the Yellow Springs, the part you had left wouldn't be of any use, would it?"

"Useless," Hui Tzu agreed.

"So," Chuang Tzu said, "I've illuminated the use of uselessness."

❧

Chuang Tzu said, "If a person *can* ramble free and easy, that person will. One who can't won't. But those who desire to leave their knight's heart hidden and leave no traces—I say to you that these just refuse the obligations of true knowledge and the full Power of Virtue. They stumble and fall without turning back, or burn on ahead like wildfire, never even looking around.

"People may stand and work together as lord and officer, but that may be just the product of a single season. In another time, they may not hold to the same distinctions. *This* is what's meant by the old saying, 'The one who's gotten there leaves no traces.'

"Admiring the past and despising the present is an affectation of scholars. Although, indeed, even one like Hsi-wei, were he to look at this present age, could hardly help but be disturbed. It is only the one who's really gotten there who can ramble free and easy in this world without sinking into the despicable, who can follow even ordinary men without losing himself. The teaching of such people is not available to scholars. Nor is it like what they teach."

❧

KEEN EYES SEE CLEARLY; KEEN EARS HEAR DISTINCTLY; A keen nose can distinguish odors, and a keen mouth, flavors. A keen heart and mind knows. Keen knowing is all there is to the Power of Virtue. Speaking of any of these, we can say that it must not be obstructed. What gets obstructed chokes, and what can't stop being choked gets stiff. Stiffness is generally bad for life.

All living things need to breathe. When they don't get enough air, it's no fault of heaven's. Heaven gave them holes and day and night provide air, but people block passages. Our flesh surrounds a multitude of cavities, and the heart rambles within them. Where there are no roomy halls, wives and mothers-in-law will get on one another's nerves. If the heart can't ramble, the senses will go to war. Forests and groves, mountains and hills—they're good for people because in them the spirit rambles unconquerably. But the power of open space is lost if we merely rush off through it in search of a name. Fame drains away into violence. Obstinacy passes for resolve. And "knowing" shows itself in the struggle of swords. Then brush grows in fields gone beyond fallow, and is jealously guarded. Is the business of government properly fulfilled in this?

In the spring rains, and the sun of that season, the grass and trees leap up almost as if in anger. Then we begin to get our sickles and hoes ready, don't we? Yet half of what we will weed away springs up again, and we do not know why that is so.

⤳

BEING STILL MENDS ILLNESSES. RUBBING MAKES OLD FOLKS feel better. Settling the heart and mind can end agitation. But although that's so, only the troubled and weary need these remedies. Whoever is at ease won't even want to talk about them. What sages use to get the people into line, the spirit being doesn't need to ask about. A sage doesn't need to ask a Worthy how he frightens people into place. A Worthy doesn't need to ask a member of the aristocracy how he imposes order on the people. A "gentleman" doesn't bother to ask the people how they get along these days.

⤳

THERE WAS A FELLOW AT THE GATE OF YEN WHO, WHEN HIS parents died, did such a good job of wasting away as a result of the mortifications of ritual mourning that he was rewarded with an official sinecure as a model of excellence. Thereafter, half the people in his neighborhood did such a good job of wasting away in mourning that they really were mortified—they died.

When Yao wanted to give All-under-heaven to Hsu Yu, Hsu Yu fled from him. When T'ang wanted to give it to Wu Kuang, Wu Kuang was enraged, and when Ch'i T'ou just *heard about it*, he went off with all of his disciples to the River K'uan, where they all stayed for three full years despite all that the lords of the earth could do to console them. Shen-t'u Ti, when he heard of the outrageous insult of such an offer, went straight off and jumped into the Yellow River.

The reason for a fish trap is the fish. When you've got the fish, you can forget the trap. The rabbit's the reason for the snare. When you have the rabbit, you can forget the snare. The meaning of the song in your heart is the reason for the words, but once you've got the meaning, you can forget the words. Where can I find someone who's forgotten the words—to have a word with?

Robber Chih

[FROM CHAPTER 29]

ONFUCIUS HAD A FRIEND NAMED LIU-HSIA CHI WHOSE younger brother was called Robber Chih. This Robber Chih had nine thousand followers behind him as he walked all over All-under-heaven, invading and ravaging the lands of feudal lords, boring through walls and smashing doors, driving off cattle and horses, and carrying off wives and daughters. In his lust for *getting*, he forgot all claims of kinship, paying no mind to his parents or brother, even refusing to make ancestral sacrifices. Wherever he went, in great states guards patrolled city walls, while in small ones people took to their strongholds. All the ordinary people suffered.

Confucius said to Liu-hsia Chi, "A father must be able to command his son. An elder brother must be able to instruct his younger brother. If this is not so, there can be no value in kinship. Now you, sir, are one of the truly talented scholar-knights of the age, and yet your younger brother is this Robber Chih, scourge of

140

All-under-heaven, and you have been unable to instruct him. I'm deeply ashamed for you. And I beg you, permit me to go speak to him on your behalf."

Liu-hsia Chi replied, "You, sir, say that a father should be able to instruct his son, and elder brother should instruct younger, but if the son doesn't listen, even if one should be as persuasive as you, there's nothing to be done. Chih is just such a man. His heart and mind are like a geyser, his will like a whirlwind. He's strong enough to oppose any man, and quick-witted enough to make an ornament of his each and every flaw. If you go along with him, he's fine. But if you go against him, he'll be easily enraged and curse you roundly. You'd better not go."

But Confucius didn't listen. With Yen Hui driving the chariot and Tzu-kung on his right, Confucius drove off to an audience with Robber Chih.

Recouping his forces on the sunny side of Mount T'ai, Robber Chih was mincing a human liver for his lunch when Confucius arrived, dismounted, and presented himself to the usher with two bows. "I am of the K'ung clan of the state of Lu. I have heard that the general is a man of lofty righteousness."

When the usher delivered the message, Robber Chih scowled, his eyes lit up like the stars, his hair standing on end so stiffly as to lift his hat from his head. "That's K'ung Ch'iu, Confucius! The artful dodger of Lu, is it? You tell him for me, 'You spout mottoes and big talk, prattling on about King Wen and King Wu, wearing that hat of yours like a branching tree, girdling yourself in a belt of ox ribs—with your multiplicity of phrases and your strangling tangle of erroneous theories! You eat without tilling. You don't weave, but are clothed. You flap your lips and drum your tongue and give birth to all sorts of *rights* and *wrongs* for the sake of deceiving the lords of All-under-heaven! You cause the scholar-knights of All-under-heaven to turn their backs on fundamentals, foolishly setting up the principle of 'filial piety' as a wedge to gain for yourself the favor of feudal lords—and wealth, and titles of nobility. Your crimes are many and great. Be quick! Go back where you came from. Before I add your liver to my lunch."

141

But Confucius sent back word, "I have the honor of being acquainted with your brother, Chi. And I beg the honor of being permitted to enter your tent."

When the usher delivered the second message, Robber Chih replied, "Bring him before me."

Confucius rushed in and, refusing the offered mat, stepped back and bowed twice.

Robber Chih was in a great rage. He stood with feet spread wide, hand on sword, glaring at Confucius before saying in a voice like the snarl of a nursing tigress, "Come forward, you! Whatever you have to say, if it agrees with me, you live; if not, you die."

"I have heard," Confucius said, "that in All-under-heaven there are three paramount virtues: to be born and grow great and tall, handsome without peer, so that young and old, noble and mean, all are pleased when they look upon him—this is called Highest Virtue. To understand the Weave of Heaven and Earth, and to have the ability to *do*, and the eloquence to speak about all things—this is called Middling Virtue. To be bold, fierce, determined, and daring, and to gather a throng of warriors to lead—this is called Lower Virtue. Whoever has the power of even one of these virtues has enough to set himself upon the South-facing Throne, and to be titled the Lonely One, sole and only emperor.

"Now, the general," he continued, "embodies all three at once. You're eight feet and two spans tall, with a face and eyes full of light. Your lips are red as cinnabar, your teeth white and regular as a string of shells. Your voice rings like the legendary Yellow Bell. And yet your only title is 'Robber Chih.' I'm deeply ashamed for you and beg to be permitted to get you a better one.

"If it's agreeable to the general," Confucius said, "to listen to his servant, his servant begs to be sent as ambassador south to the lands of Wu and Yueh, north to the realms of Ch'i and Lu, east to the states of Sung and Wei, and west to Ch'in and Ch'u, to get them to build you a wall of several hundred *li*, and establish there a capital of several tens of myriads of people, where you will be honored as one among the feudal lords. You will give All-under-heaven a new birth, disarming and disbanding your troops, gathering and nurturing your brothers and kin, and together with them performing the sacrifices due your ancestors as the founding ancestors of a state. This is worthy, knightly behavior, and the answer to the dreams of All-under-heaven."

"Come here, *Ch'iu*," Robber Chih spat. "Those who can be ruled by thoughts of profit or reformed by admonishments are all what I'd call low, mean, benighted people. The fact that I'm big and good looking, that people sigh in their hearts when they see me, that's all just inherited straight from my mother and father. You didn't tell me that. Did you think I didn't know? I've also heard it said that people who are addicted to praising you to your face will tear you down when your back is turned. Now, you, *Ch'iu*, offer me a big walled town full of people, thinking to rule *me* with thoughts of profit—as if I were a common fool. How long could I keep the place? As big a city as it might be, there's no city equal to All-under-heaven. Yao and Shun held All-under-heaven, but their sons and grandsons didn't hold on to enough ground to stick an awl in. T'ang and Wu each stood as the Son of Heaven, but their descendants have been totally annihilated. Wasn't that precisely because they had profited so much?

"I've heard that in ancient times," Robber Chih continued, "when beasts were many and people few, that people lived in nests in trees to escape them. They ate acorns and chestnuts by day and perched in the trees at night. That's why they were known as the Nesters. They didn't even know about clothes. In the summer, they collected firewood to burn in the winter. So they were called People Who Know How to Live. In the time of Shen Nung, who invented farming, they slept easy when they lay down and stayed wide awake when they rose. They knew who their mothers were, but not their fathers. They lived with herds of elk and deer and they tilled to eat and wove to be clothed without any thought of doing harm to anyone. And so it went, until the time of the Yellow Emperor, who wasn't able to *get there* to the Power of Virtue. When he waged war on Ch'ih Yu in the wilds of Cho-lu, blood flowed over a hundred *li*. Then Yao and Shun really did it, setting up a herd of ministers! T'ang banished his master, Chieh. And King Wu murdered his sovereign, Chou, the last king of the Shang. And from that time on, the strong have abused the weak, and the many have mobbed the few. Since the era of T'ang and Wu, they may all be counted among the hosts of chaos.

"Now you come along, preaching the 'Tao' of Wen and Wu, making use of All-under-heaven with your handmade robes and your narrow girdle, with your pretty speeches and false ways, to deceive and confuse the rulers of All-under-heaven, hoping to get rich and powerful. There's no greater robber than you! Why is it that in All-under-heaven they don't just give you the title of 'Robber Ch'iu' while they call me Robber Chih? You and your sweet phrases made Tzu-lu follow you, putting aside his helmet and long sword to follow your teaching. And All-under-heaven declared, 'That K'ung Ch'iu! He can stop violence and prohibit wrongdoing!' But it killed *him*. When Tzu-lu wanted to kill that Prince of Wei and didn't get the job done, they hanged his pickled corpse out on top of Wei's East Gate. That's where your teaching will get you. You call yourself a scholar-knight of talent, or a sage? You've twice been driven from Lu. You had to cover your tracks when you left Wei. You were in dire straits in Ch'i, and they surrounded you on the border between Ch'en and Ts'ai. You're not welcome anywhere in All-under-heaven. You taught Tzu-lu how to get pickled. This two-hearted calamity of yours—at its best, it does nothing for you, and at its worst, it does nothing for anyone. What's worth honoring about this 'Tao' you embrace?

"Of all the high ones in all the world, there's none like the Yellow Emperor. And yet even the Yellow Emperor could not encompass the Power of Virtue. He made war at Cho-lu, and the earth ran with blood for a hundred *li*. Yao was uncaring toward his children. Shun was unfilial. Yu got a withered side. T'ang banished his own lord. King Wu murdered Chou. King Wen got himself imprisoned at Yu-li. All these men are esteemed, held high by the world, but who could work this through without seeing that what they really did was throw their 'truth' into doubt and go against their own natures—and all for the sake of profit?

144

"Who does the world call 'worthy knights'? Po Yi and Shu Ch'i—but Po Yi and Shu Ch'i threw away the lordship of Ku-chu and chose to starve to death on Mount Shouyang. Their flesh and bones went unburied.

"Pao Chiao made good conduct his only adornment," Robber Chih continued, "but when he realized that even the acorns he ate 'belonged' to some lord of the world, he embraced a tree until he starved. When Shen-t'u Ti offered admonishment no one would listen to, he loaded a boulder in his pack and jumped into the river to feed the fish and turtles. Chieh Tzu-t'ui got all the way to loyalty. He sliced his own thigh to feed Duke Wen. But then, when Duke Wen turned his back on him, he went off in a rage and hugged some tree while the forest burned around him. When the girl Wei Sheng had sworn to meet under the bridge didn't show up, and the water rose to meet him instead, he kept his appointment and died there, embracing a pillar of the bridge. These four were no different than road-kill—flattened dogs, pigs fleeing the slaughterer, beggars with their alms gourds. They were all so caught up in getting a *name* that they took life itself lightly, forgetting that they must first nurture their bodies if they would live long.

"Who does the world call loyal? There's none to match Prince Pi-kan and Wu Tzu-hsu. Wu was thrown into the river to drown. Pi-kan had his heart cut out. They name them 'loyal ministers,' but in fact, they should be called the laughingstock of All-under-heaven. From the highest down to Wu Tzu-hsu and Pi-kan, there's not a one worth a string of shells. If you want to tell me ghost stories, I don't know anything about that. But if you want to tell me about human affairs—and tell me nothing but these—I've heard it all. I know it all. Now *I'll* tell *you* about how humans feel. Their eyes want to see colors. Their ears want to hear sounds. Their mouths want to taste flavors. They want to be filled with what their *ch'i* and their hearts desire. People at best live to a hundred. They hope for eighty, or at least sixty, years. Take away time spent sick or recovering, nursing the dying or mourning the dead, or time worrying over one thing or another, and times between, when you can actually open your mouth and laugh out loud—in a month, not more than five or six days. Heaven and earth are endless, but humankind lives only a single season. To take the tool for one season's labor to a task that's endless—it's gone more quickly than a galloping horse past a crack in the wall. If you can't get your way and live your fated years—that's not knowing Tao. I reject *all* your words, *Ch'iu.* Go now. Go back to where you came from. Say no more. Your 'Tao' is the froth of madness, a cunning, artful, empty, artificial business. There's nothing of the truth in it. It's not even worth working through."

Confucius bowed twice and rushed out the door. When he mounted his chariot, he dropped the reins three times. His eyes blinded, he couldn't see a thing. His face was ashen as he leaned on the cross bar and bowed his head, unable to gather any *ch'i* at all.

When he got back to the east gate of the city wall of Lu, he ran into Liu-hsia Chi, who remarked, "I haven't seen you for days now. Your chariot and horses are colored with road dust. I catch a hint of you having gone to see Chih, do I?"

Confucius looked up into the heavens and sighed. "That's so."

"And did he reject your views, as I suggested he might?"

"It's so. You might even say old Ch'iu burned the medicinal moxa on his own flesh without even waiting to get sick. Or that it was sick to rush off to pat the tiger's head and tie a pigtail in his whiskers. How did I escape his jaws?"

Speaking of Swords

[CHAPTER 30]

IN THE OLD DAYS, KING WEN OF CHAO DELIGHTED IN swordsmanship. Swordsmen crowded around his gates and he had
more than three thousand of them as retainers. Day and night,
they came before him to have at each other, and the harvest of
killed and wounded exceeded a hundred per year. But he loved it
relentlessly, and within three years the whole country was in decline, and neighboring feudal lords all began plotting and schem-
ing against it.

Crown Prince Kuei, seeing the calamity, summoned his retinue
together and said, "I'll give a thousand in gold to anyone who can
convince the king to stop all this swordplay."

The retainers replied, "Chuang Tzu can do it!"

So the crown prince sent one of his men to take a thousand in
gold to Chuang Tzu. But the master declined the offer, returning
with the man nevertheless for an audience with the crown
prince.

"What do you ask of me that I should be rewarded with a thousand in gold?"

"I've heard you are an enlightened sage, and I, your humble follower, humbly sent a thousand in gold to support your entourage. If you are unwilling to accept it, how could I dare speak more of it?"

"I've heard that the crown prince wishes to use me," Chuang Tzu said, "to cut off the king's delight and his addiction. But if you send me up to speak before the king, and I offend him, I will have failed you as well, and this body will be punished to death. What use will I have for gold then? And if I meet your end through speaking up, what in the land of Chao might I ask for that would not be granted?"

"That's so," the crown prince said. "But our king gives audience only to swordsmen."

"No problem," Chuang Tzu said. "I'm *good* on swords."

"Good. But all the swordsmen who are granted an audience with the king have hair like brambles and bristling beards," the prince replied. "They wear loose caps with coarse straps dangling, and robes cut short behind. They glare and tell war stories, and the king loves it. If you go to an audience dressed like one of those Confucian weaklings, you'll certainly offend him."

"If it please your highness, I'll submit to being dressed to kill."

Over the following three days, Chuang Tzu got "dressed fit to kill" like a swordsman, then sought audience with the crown prince. The crown prince escorted him to an audience with the king. The king bared his sword's white blade as he awaited them. Chuang Tzu entered the palace doorway unhurriedly, and when he saw the king, he didn't bow.

The king demanded, "What have you got to show me now that you've gotten the crown prince to put you forward?"

"I've heard the Great King delights in swords, so I've brought mine to the king's audience."

"And what special powers have you with the sword?"

"My sword? Put a man against me and my sword, one at every

148

ten paces, and we'll stroll through them for a thousand *li* without pausing."

The king was impressed. "There's no match for you in All-under-heaven!"

"To make use of the sword," Chuang Tzu said, "first make an empty feint. Then open your opponent by giving him an obvious advantage. Then strike, and get there first. But let me demonstrate."

"You, sir, go and take your rest in your quarters," the king said. "Await my command. When the show is arranged, I will call for you."

For seven days, the king held combat. Some sixty swordsmen were killed or wounded. He finally chose five or six to submit themselves and their swords to the test before the court. Then he summoned Chuang Tzu. "Today we'll show these knights some honest swordsmanship," he smiled.

"I've been waiting for this," Chuang Tzu replied.

"Long sword or short, sir?" the king asked.

"Oh, any kind will do," Chuang Tzu smiled. "In fact, I brought three that might be fit for a king. If you don't mind, I'll speak of them before submitting them to the test. I have the Sword of the Son of Heaven, the Sword of the Feudal Lord, and the sword of the ordinary man."

"What's this Sword of the Son of Heaven like?" the king demanded.

"The Sword of the Son of Heaven takes the valley and the great stone wall of the state of Yen as its point, the realms of Ch'i and Tai for its blade, the lands of Chin and Way for its forte and foible. The states of Chou and Sung are its hilt, and Han and Wei are its pommel. It's securely wrapped by the four barbarian tribes and tied with the string of the Four Seasons. Its scabbard is the Sea of Po, and its belt is the Mountain of the Enduring Heart. The Five Elements give it order, and the example of the Power of Virtue provides its judgments. Yin and Yang draw this blade. Spring and summer grasp it. Autumn and winter are its use. Thrust, and nothing stands before it; parry high and none will rise above it;

parry low, and nothing will get beneath it; parry to the side, and none will get around it. Above, it slices floating clouds; below, it pierces the stolid earth. Use this sword but once, and the feudal lords will see their master and All-under-heaven will submit. Such is the Sword of the Son of Heaven."

King Wen looked confused, as if he'd lost a trial with himself. "And the Sword of the Feudal Lord," he asked, "what about that?"

"The Sword of the Feudal Lord has knowing and courageous knights for its point, pure and chaste knights for its blade, worthy and excellent knights for its forte and foible, loyal and sage knights as its hilt, and bold warriors and bravos as its pommel. Thrust with this sword, and nothing stands before it. Parry high, and none will outreach it; parry low, and none will get under it; parry to the side, and none will get around it. Its highest reach rounds the heavens, following the lead of sun, moon, and stars. Its lowest reach squares with the earth, following the Four Seasons. In the middle it harmonizes with the song in the hearts of the people, bringing peace to every village. Use *this* sword but once, and in the shudder of the thunderbolt there will be none who do not submit to hear and abide by the commands of the lord. This is the Sword of the Feudal Lord."

"And what about the sword of the ordinary man?" King Wen asked.

"The swords of ordinary men—men with hair like brambles and with bristling beards? Loose-capped, with coarse straps dangling, with robes cut short behind? The kind that glare and relish telling war stories? That sword, when it thrusts, is met with a thrust. Parry high with it, and it lets in a sweep that lops heads from necks. Parry low, and it lets in a thrust that pierces liver or lung. Those who would strike with the sword of an ordinary man are nothing but fighting cocks. One morning they crow. One word from you, and they'll croak. They're no use to your realm. Now a Great King has the standing to become the Son of Heaven, yet *you* are addicted to the swords of ordinary men. Your servant dares to suggest that this is unworthy of you."

150

The king took Chuang Tzu in hand and led him into the High Hall. The chief chef prepared a meal, but the king just circled around it.

"Oh, Great King," Chuang Tzu urged, "sit quiet. Settle your *ch'i*. The sword business is done."

The king remained inside the palace for three months. The swordsmen submitted themselves to their swords in their own chambers.

The Old Fisherman

[CHAPTER 31]

CONFUCIUS WENT TO STROLL IN BLACK CURTAIN GROVE. When he got to the knoll called the Apricot Altar, he sat down to rest. His disciples dug out their books while he fingered his lute and sang. He wasn't half through his song when an old fisherman appeared, climbed from his boat, and approached. His beard and brows were turning white, his hair hanging uncombed down his back, his broad sleeves flapping. He came up the bank and stopped when he got to dry ground. With his left hand on his knee and his right propping his chin, he listened. When the piece ended, he called to Tzu-kung and Tzu-lu, and the two disciples approached him. He pointed at Confucius and asked, "What does *he* do?"

"He's a gentleman from the state of Lu," Tzu-lu replied. When asked to which clan the master belonged, Tzu-lu answered, "He's a K'ung."

"This Mr. K'ung—what's his calling?"

152

Tzu-lu hadn't yet formulated his answer when Tzu-kung spoke up. "Master K'ung's nature is submissive to the principle of loyalty and to his standing by his word. He himself practices benevolence and righteousness, refines and perfects rites and music, and identifies what is proper in human relationships. Loyal to his lord above him, he passes down means of transformation, to the profit of all. Such is the calling of Master K'ung."

"Is he a lord, with lands?"

"No."

"Is he an officer of some king or feudal lord?"

"No," Tzu-kung answered again.

The visitor laughed as he turned to go, saying, "Benevolence, eh? Benevolence. But I'm afraid he won't get out alive. To embitter the heart and mind and belabor the form, to walk his truth along a cliff like this . . . woo-hoo! He's split a long way from the Tao."

When Tzu-kung reported back to Confucius, the master put aside his lute, jumped up and said, "He's a sage!" Confucius went down after him, arriving at the edge of the marsh just as the old man was grasping his pole and pulling his boat back into the water. Looking over his shoulder and seeing Confucius, he came back and stood before him. Confucius backed away, then, after bowing twice, came forward again.

"What do you want?" the fisherman asked.

"Just now," Confucius said, "the elder made some rather mysterious remarks, and then departed. Unworthy, I don't understand your meaning. I humbly await the fresh breeze of your attention. If you will favor me with the sound of your voice, I might yet learn something."

"Ho! Deep indeed is your addiction to learning!"

Confucius bowed twice again, and when he rose, said, "From my youth until this very day, I have cultivated learning—sixty-nine years. But I haven't yet heard the teaching that *gets there*. Dare I listen with other than an open mind and heart?"

"Birds of a feather flock together, and all sing the same song. It's a principle of nature," the old fisherman said. "So if I may, I'll

153

put aside my concerns and take up yours. You're interested in the affairs of people—the Son of Heaven, feudal lords, high officers of state, and ordinary people. When these four hold themselves upright, that's attractive government. If the four get away from their proper standing, nothing could create greater disorder. When officials attend to their charges and ordinary folks take care of business, nothing can get out of order.

"Fields lost in weeds and leaking roofs; not enough clothes or food; nothing set aside as tax time arrives; wives and concubines in disharmony; old and young in disorder—these are the sorrows of ordinary folks.

"Insufficient ability to master their responsibilities; official business that is ungovernable; deportment that's not clear and clean; herds of underlings who are careless and wild; not getting merit or praise or not being rewarded with rank and pay—these are the sorrows of high officers of state.

"Courts where there are no loyal ministers; great families of the realm in dark disorder; craftsmen without appreciable skills producing unattractive objects unfit for tribute to the Overlord; getting put back in the ranks at the spring and autumn levies, or not gaining the good grace of the Son of Heaven—these are the sorrows of the feudal lord.

"Yin and yang out of harmony; unseasonable cold and heat damaging a multitude of things; feudal lords who are violent and disorderly and presumptuously attack one another, chopping up people in the process; rites and music improperly performed; constantly running short of funds; human relationships in disarray, and the common people behaving lewdly—these are the sorrows of the Son of Heaven.

"Now you're not a prince, or a marquis, or a steward," the old fisherman continued, "you're not even a high minister with administrative duties. Yet you want to 'refine and perfect rites and music,' and 'identify what is proper in human relationships.' Isn't that a pretty tall order of business?

"Humanity is afflicted with eight blemishes, and in handling business there are four calamities. These demand close examination. When someone does something that's none of his business, that's called excessive. To bring up topics no one has mentioned is called artful insinuating. To permit another's ideas to change your speech is fawning. To speak without distinguishing right from wrong is simpering flattery. To love talking about other people's moral weakness is called slander. To break up friendships and drive a wedge between relatives is called being worse than a thief. To praise or blame falsely for any purpose is shameful wickedness. Without regard to right or wrong, to try to face both ways at once and to use the desires of others against them is called treachery. In the world outside, these eight afflictions spread chaos among people; within the self, they inflict deep wounds. No gentleman will befriend one who engages in them, nor will any lord employ such a one.

"As for the four calamities," the old fisherman continued, "being addicted to undertaking great projects and changing simple, constant ways for the sake of heaping up the dirt of merit and fame—this is called ambition; to monopolize knowledge and insist upon having your own way, and misappropriating others' things for your own benefit is called avarice; to see your own excesses while refusing to change, or to listen to reproof only to grow worse, is called deaf obstinacy; to praise those who agree with you only to refuse to see any good, even when it's there, in those who differ is called boastful egotism. These are the four calamities. If you can get away from the eight afflictions and stay away from the four calamities, you might begin to be teachable."

Confucius looked crestfallen. He sighed, and after bowing twice again, said, "I've been driven twice from Lu. I had to cover my trail when I left Wei. In Sung, they cut down a tree on me. I was surrounded on the border between Ch'en and Ts'ai. I don't know how I've lost out. What could it have been that led to those four misunderstandings?"

The fisherman's expression turned chilly. "It's extremely . . . how very difficult it is to get you to look within yourself! There once was a man who feared his own shadow and who hated his footprints and tried to escape from them. The more he lifted his feet, the more tracks he made. As fast as he could go, his shadow remained with him. Thinking he was still going too slow, he streaked like an arrow until all his strength was spent, and he died. He didn't realize that sitting in the shade of a tree would do away with his shadow, and living quietly would leave his traces to fade away. Stupid. Extremely stupid.

"Now you, sir, you examine benevolence and righteousness. You search the boundaries between same and different. You examine the turnings of stillness and movement. You establish rules for giving and receiving. You make principles out of love and hate, and harmonize occasions for happiness and anger. And yet these mechanisms of yours have failed to save you. Just take care of *yourself.* Just hold to the truth of your heart, and hand *things* back to others, then there will be nothing to bind you. You're not taking care of yourself, and yet you're trying to get others to do so. Isn't that superficial?"

Again, Confucius looked crestfallen. "What do you mean," he asked, "when you say 'the truth in your heart'?"

"Truth?" the old fisherman asked. "Getting to purity and sincerity. If you're not pure and not sincere, you can't move people. Fake tears and wailing may appear sorrowful, but they don't make real mourning. Fake anger may make you seem stern, but it doesn't produce awe. Fake affection, and you'll get smiles, but no harmony. True sorrow can mourn without a sound. True anger can be awesome even before it's visible. True affection brings harmony even before it brings a smile. When truth is inside, the spirit can move abroad. That's the noble value of truth.

"It has uses when dealing with people: in serving loved ones, it is kindness and devotion; in serving the ruler, it is loyalty and straightforwardness; at a drinking party, it's joyful merriment; at a funeral, it is sorrowful mourning. The purpose of loyalty and straightforwardness is meritorious service. The purpose of a drinking party is merriment. The purpose of funerals is the expression of sorrow. The purpose of serving loved ones is their comfort. The most elegant plan for achieving all this meritorious accomplishment doesn't involve following any single set of foot-

156

prints. When you comfort your loved ones, there's no need to theorize about means; joyful drinking doesn't require quibbling about the cups; to express sorrowful mourning, there's no need to look up appropriate ritual. Rituals are created by our contemporaries. Truth comes from heaven. It is exactly as it is, and you can't change it. So the sage follows heaven as surely as water flows downhill and finds value only in truth. He doesn't get snared in the grasp of custom.

"The stupid run against this, " he continued. "They can't follow heaven. Their hearts overflowing with 'humanity,' they don't know the value of truth and so they follow along after every change in custom, and never get enough. It's so sad that you fell into the mire of human deceit so young, and have heard the great Tao so late."

Confucius bowed twice again, rose, and said, "But now I've attained it, it's a blessing from heaven. Oh, elder, if you wouldn't consider it disgraceful to permit me to submit myself as your disciple, and to teach me yourself . . . I ask where you live and beg to be permitted to take on the great task of learning, at last, the Great Tao."

The old fisherman replied, "I've heard it said, 'If you *can* go along with someone, do—all the way to the mystery of Tao. If you can't, if he doesn't know the way, take true care not to go with him, and you will remain blameless.' You keep at it. I must leave you now. I must leave you." Setting his pole, he pushed off, slipping among green reeds.

Yen Hui had brought the chariot around, and Tzu-lu reached the mounting strap toward Confucius. But he didn't even turn toward them. He stood waiting until the waves had settled in the wake and the sound of poling faded away. Only then did he dare mount.

Tzu-lu, sitting beside him, said, "I have been your disciple for a long time, for sure, but I've never until now seen the master treat a chance encounter with such reverence. Masters of ten thousand chariots, lords of a thousand, when they give you audience, always seat you on a level with themselves and treat you with the ritual due an equal, while you remain haughty and aloof. Now some old fisherman comes up and leans on his pole in your face, and you bend yourself into the shape of a chiming stone with your bowing and scraping every time you respond to him. Isn't this too much? All your disciples think it's strange. What's this old fisherman done to deserve it?"

Confucius leaned forward on the chariot bar, sighed, and said, "Hard. You're very hard to change, Tzu-lu. All this immersion in ritual and righteousness hasn't yet managed to send off your slavish, petty heart. Look here. I'll tell you. To meet an elder and fail to show respect is to fail at ritual. To see a worthy and not honor him is to lack benevolence. If that man was not one who's *gotten there*, he wouldn't be able to make people bow and scrape. And if the people who bow down don't do it with their very essence, they can't gain the truth, and they will be eternally wounding themselves. Alas, there's nothing worse than a lack of benevolence toward others, and you, Tzu-lu, my follower, choose that for yourself.

"Now, the Tao is that of which all the ten thousand things are followers. All things that get it live; all things that lose it die. To turn from it in your work is to be defeated; to follow it is completion. So: where there is Tao, the sage reveres it. This fisherman and Tao—you could say he owns it. How would I dare not show him respect?"

Glossary

This glossary provides some information about names, both personal and geographical, mentioned in this translation of *Chuang Tzu*. We hope it will help readers distinguish between real historical people and places, mythical people and places, and ad hoc creations of this most imaginative of authors. Any names not found here may be safely assumed to be those of either purely fictional characters, or of minor historical characters used by the author to give a patina of historicity to his fictional enterprises.

In addition to names, we offer some definition and explanation of a few important terms and repeated themes, and an occasional comment on word play, both apparent puns and graphic play made possible by the nature of the Chinese characters. Unless they are mentioned more than once in the work, we will not generally identify figures whose only intended function is obviously rhetorical.

Ch'ang Chi   The historical man behind this name was recognized as a more or less undistinguished disciple of the historical K'ung Ch'iu, known in the West as Confucius. In reading *Chuang Tzu*, however, it's essential to remember that the personal characterizations of figures like Ch'ang Chi are first and foremost fictional constructions of Chuang Tzu.

CH'ANG HUNG   A high official in the reign of one of the kings of the Chou dynasty (until the Ch'in dynasty [221–206 BCE], earthly, as opposed to mythical or supernatural rulers, were referred to as kings rather than as emperors). Context clearly indicates his intended function in the text.

CHAO WEN   The legendary and perhaps also historical master of the instrument usually translated as *lute* (sometimes as *zither*). The lute of Chuang Tzu's time was probably fairly closely related to the modern *ch'in*, an instrument very closely related to the Japanese *koto*. Some *ch'in* music and a lot of *koto* music is readily available on record, tape, or CD, for those who'd like to get and inkling of what Chuang Tzu was thinking of, or remembering, as he made this reference.

CH'EN AND TS'AI   These were petty feudal states in the Spring and Autumn period of the Chou dynasty. They are famous primarily for rejecting Confucius, who was, at the time, a politically dangerous guest.

CH'I   A strong North China state in the Spring and Autumn period. It had more or less collapsed by Chuang Tzu's time.

CH'I-CHI AND HUA-LIU   These horses, credited with running a thousand *li* (one third of a mile to the *li*) in a day, certainly qualify for mythical, not just legendary, status.

CHI CH'U   A mythical culture hero, not quite on a par with Fu Hsi, whose exploits are noted later in this glossary.

CHIEH   Also called Chieh Kuei, he is perhaps the last historical ruler of the first Chinese dynasty, the Hsia, which—although long regarded as legendary in the West—has lately been finding supporters as an identifiable stage in the historical development of China, if not as a "dynasty." He is the first of the "bad last" rulers made necessary in traditional Chinese historiography by the ideological position that says legitimacy ("The Mandate of Heaven") has a moral base. If he was overthrown by the founder of the Shang dynasty (the agreed-upon "first historical dynasty"), he *must* have been evil. Presented as a paragon of arrogance, brutality, and lust, he was nonetheless only

160

sent into exile by the founder of Shang. Kuan Lung-feng, mentioned as having been murdered by him, had remonstrated when Chieh's abominable behavior (hot yang sexuality) caused two important rivers to dry up in shame.

CHOU   There are several. In Chinese, because their names are, in most cases, written with different characters, it's less confusing than it may be in English. The Chou mentioned in the same breath with Chieh of the Hsia is Chou Hsin, the "bad last" ruler of Shang. Sexual misbehavior, specifically over attentiveness to a concubine, was, as with Chieh, a prominent factor in his evil reputation. At the request of his favorite, T'a Chi, he reportedly had built a pleasure grounds stocked with ponds of wine and featuring naked people hanging from the trees. When King Wu, founder of the Chou dynasty (a different character is used for *this* Chou) overthrew him, he had Chou's own palace burned down around him. Too much yang, aided and abetted by too much yin, in the person of the concubine, causes the immorality that brings the downfall of the realm. The Chinese character *chou* used as the name of the dynasty (mentioned immediately above), in which Chuang Tzu lived and wrote, is, perhaps not merely coincidentally, also the character used for Chuang Tzu's personal name.

CHUANG CHOU   Also called Chuang Tzu, or Master Chuang, was the presumed author of the book called *Chuang Tzu*. His dates are now thought to have been in the latter half of the fourth century BCE. The character written to represent the syllable *Chuang* shows a strong man hiding under some leaves. Without the leaves, the remainder of the character means strong, robust, mature, in the prime of life. In modern Chinese, and most likely for quite a long time, the three stages of human life have been called *ch'ing nian* (the green years), *chuang nian* (the prime of life), and *lao nian* (the aged years). Readers of this book will doubtless recognize the *lao* of *lao nian* as the *lao* in the name Lao Tzu, the author of the other main Taoist classic, the *Tao Te Ching*. If the various Chuang Tzus presented here, from the "real" Chuang Tzu, the witty author of the "Inner Chapters" (1-7), to the fictional sword-fighting Chuang Tzu of chapter 30, share one thing, it is precisely the vigor of a human being in the prime of life, just as the words of Lao Tzu are clearly representative of the wisdom of age. Chuang Tzu's personal name, Chou, is the same as the name of the dynasty he lived under. Chuang Tzu is certainly representative of the prime of life of Chou culture, whether the pun works or not. Pseudonyms were common among Chinese authors, and if Chuang Tzu were a conscious pseudonym, it would help account for the lack of actual historical information about the author. Incidentally, although Lao Tzu is mentioned in the *Chuang Tzu* , and several lines that appear in the *Tao Te Ching* also appear here, some scholars believe it's likely that the *Chuang Tzu* actually existed as a complete text before the *Tao Te Ching.*

CH'UI Sometimes referred to as Craftsman Ch'ui, the mythical inventor of the carpenter's compass and square, emblematic of the damage done to nature by even the most fundamental technological advances.

CONFUCIUS Born in the state of Lu, Master K'ung, K'ung Ch'iu (551–479 BCE), was one of the world's great teachers. His importance is attested to by the fact that Chuang Tzu makes him the focal point of many of his wittiest sallies. It should be noted that the Chuang Tzu version of Confucius is almost always satirical, and most often wholly fictitious. In the Robber Chih story, Robber Chih refers to the master by his personal name, Ch'iu, something that would have been unthinkable even in Confucius's own time, and something almost, if not quite, sacrilegious, by the time the Robber Chih chapter was written. On the other hand, it should be noted that the Confucius of the "Inner Chapters" (the first seven) is treated pretty gently, and even in the later chapters he is given quite a few good lines. His followers are uniformly given a good going-over, however.

DUKE HUAN Ruler of the feudal state of Ch'i (reigned 685–643 BCE), he was the first of five "hegemons" to dominate China, without formally overthrowing the Chou dynasty, during the era known as the Spring and Autumn period (722–481 BCE). Kuan Chung was his prime minister.

DUKE WEI This may be the historical son of Duke Huan.

FU HSI The first of the five mythical rulers, a culture hero, he invented—among many other things—hunting, fishing, the tending of flocks, musical instruments, and the eight original trigrams from which the *I Ching*, or *Classic of Change,* was later constructed.

HANTAN Capital of the feudal state of Chao; its people affected a stylish walk.

Glossary

HAO A small state in east central China.

HEART AND MIND The single character we translate as "heart and mind" is the character *hsin*, in early forms a recognizable picture of a human heart. Any understanding of the meaning of the word is complicated by the fact that in some periods of early Chinese history, it was assumed that the heart was the organ of mental activity. People of European culture generally think of the *mind* as the organ of intellectual activity, and locate it in the brain. We believe that Chuang Tzu conceives of mental activity as properly involving both reason and emotion, logic and intuition. The word *hsin*, "heart," is also often interpreted by Chinese philosophers as a shorthand for *hsing*, "nature." Chuang Tzu appears to believe that it is in our natures to apprehend reality with both the heart and the mind at once.

HSI SHIH Woman of legendary beauty.

HUAN TOU A minister under the legendary first Sage Emperor, Yao, he makes several appearances in the Confucian *Shu Ching*, "Classic of History." He was banished during the period when the second Sage Emperor, Shun, ruled in conjunction with Yao.

HUI TZU Hui Shih, or Master Hui, was a historical person and a contemporary of the historical Chuang Tzu. He was the most important figure in the school of the logicians or sophists. Chuang Tzu's sarcastic treatment of Hui Tzu as a man bound up in the spider web of words is tinctured by an appreciation of his intellect and wit. A real human friendship, and not merely an intellectual competition, appears to lie at the foundation of Chuang Tzu's depiction.

JAN CH'IU Also known as Tzu Yu, he was a disciple of Confucius. In the *Book of Mencius*, Confucius is quoted as cursing Jan Ch'iu for his mistreatment of the people during his service as an official of a great family. The character presented here by Chuang Tzu seems stiff and a little less than straightforward. Considering Jan Ch'iu's later career, it may be that Chuang Tzu is also satirizing Confucius's rather gnomic teaching style here as well.

KING WEN The Cultured King, sometimes called simply Wen, he was the ruler of the Chou state before it supplanted the Shang dynasty. According to Confucian mythology, it was his civil (*wen*) virtue that achieved the Mandate of Heaven for his house. The sword-worshipping King of Wen of chapter 30 was a petty kinglet of the Warring States period (480–222 BCE).

KING WU   The Martial King, he was the eldest son of King Wen of Chou. He conquered Shang and established the Chou dynasty by force of arms. The play between *wen* and *wu*, the civil and military virtues, is a major theme of Chinese mythology.

KUAN CHUNG   *See* Duke Huan. Kuan Chung's thought was associated with the development of Legalism, a school of totalitarian political philosophy that reached its highest point only after Chuang Tzu's death. Chuang Tzu would have abhorred the Legalists' approach to government, and his portrayal of Kuan Chung as dismally stupid is likely a fair indication of his presentiments about Kuan's philosophy. The historical Confucius admired Kuan Chung, while Mencius, the great Confucian who was nearly a contemporary of Chuang Tzu, also despised him. He is regarded as China's first economist.

KUAN LUNG-FENG   A virtuous minister of Chieh, the "last bad" ruler of the Hsia dynasty.

KUAN YIN (BORDER GUARD)   He was the person credited with coercing Lao Tzu into writing down the *Tao Te Ching* (to earn passage through the pass). This original legend helps remedy the silly spectacle of the man who said, "He who knows does not speak," writing a book on the Way.

K'UANG   A music master, he was already legendary in Chuang Tzu's time.

K'UN-LUN   Mythical peak and mountain range to the west of China, where the goddess called Queen Mother of the West was believed to dwell. Identified with the Himalayas.

LAO TZU   Also known in the *Chuang Tzu* as Lao Tan and as Lao Lai-tzu, he was the legendary author of the *Tao Te Ching*. Quotations from Lao Tzu that also occur in the *Tao Te Ching* are found in chapters 3, 5, 7, 11, 22, and 26.

LIANG   Located on the middle reaches of the Yellow River in the North China Plain.

LIEH TZU   The third of the famous Taoists after Lao Tzu and Chuang Tzu, Master Lieh is seen here in several different lights. He rides the wind, but as Chuang Tzu suggests, he seems to find it hard to get beyond that sort of magic. In a few anecdotes he is, maybe, a wise man. In some he is, perhaps, a fool. A number of puns throughout the book having to do with the perils of discipleship are culminated in the story about Lieh Tzu and *his* master, Winepot, when the master suggests that Lieh Tzu follow the fleeing shaman/physiognomist. The eponymous book attributed to him is a late compilation, containing, among other things, most of the Lieh Tzu stories from Chuang Tzu.

LU   In the southwest of the Shantung peninsula, this small, culturally conservative feudal state was the birthplace of Confucius. Growing up and taking up his vocation as a teacher there, he also served in the government (and was driven into exile) at least twice.

MAO CH'IANG   As the text notes, she was a legendary beauty. In most cases where the text defines the function of a name, we have not included the name in the glossary. Here we grant her equal time with her rival, Hsi Shih.

MASTER WINEPOT   Lieh Tzu's master is a fictional creation of Chuang Tzu. The name has been previously translated as Master Pot, or left in transliteration as Hu Tzu, but it seems clear that Chuang Tzu wants to portray Lieh Tzu as the disciple of a Winepot. The passage begins with Lieh Tzu's intoxication with the powers of the shaman physiognomist; the word for "drunkenness" is used only one other time in the entire book (perhaps tellingly, in the passage in which Kuan Yin compares alcoholic and true enlightenment). The word *hu*, meaning explicitly "*wine*pot," is found in the poetry of both T'ao Ch'ien and Li Po, and the two famous poets were both drinkers and Taoists. The potentially ironic link between chemical and spiritual intoxication, drunkenness and enlightenment, was no more lost on Chuang Tzu than on these poets.

MIN TZU   Min Tzu-ch'ien was a disciple of Confucius. He is said by Mencius to be an equal of Yen Hui, Confucius's favorite, as an exemplar of virtuous conduct.

MO TZU   Mo Ti was the historical founder (fourth century BCE) of a religion based on universal love, economy in ritual, and belief in a hereafter. His followers are called Mohists. *See* Yang Chu.

NONDOING   Not *not doing*, but doing without ado. The ability to accomplish through nondoing is in the nature of the sage. For the Taoist, it is achieved through meditation, "sitting forgetting," which, in allowing the meditator to be free of words, puts him or her in identity with Tao. Nondoing is, thus, perfect doing, doing without effort or interest, without beginning or end, in the manner of Tao itself. It comes naturally to all beings, but must be unlearned, by forgetting, by those who have forgotten how to nondo. It is doing the best you can in a paradoxical sense: What is beyond the facts and your fate, you can't do; anything else you can do without overdoing is your best, even if it's not very good.

NORTH SEA JO   God of the Northern Sea (that is, the Yellow Sea, east of North China, into which the Yellow River flows). Something amazingly close to the Jo-Joe pun we offer here is in the original, where the name of the god is repeated as an element of the next phrase, making fun of the snobbishness of the *relatively* enlightened. Chuang Tzu appears to share Shakespeare's infamous willingness to risk the world for the sake of a pun.

P'ENG   One of the truly great imaginative creations of Chuang Tzu. The modern Chinese character consists of a phonetic element, which gives the pronunciation, and a signific element, which means "bird," the conventional interpretation being that it is the bird (signified) whose name is pronounced *p'eng*, like the phonetic element. But the phonetic element itself was originally used to stand for the bird's name, and the character formed by that phonetic standing alone is clearly a drawing of a very large bird in the earliest script. Its alternative and now dominant meaning is also "friend," "companion," or "match." Chuang Tzu is "of a feather" with this bird.

P'ENG TZU   There is considerable disagreement about the age of this celebrated Chinese version of Methuselah.

PI KAN   A historical figure, Pi Kan appears several times in the *Book of Documents*. He was a loyal minister of Chou Hsin (aka Shou), the "last bad" king of the Shang. Chuang Tzu sets the pattern for the traditional Chinese historical worldview here, finding both nobility and stupidity in a loyalty that is fatal.

PO LO   A legendary horseman, judge of horseflesh, and trainer of exceptional steeds. In a culture where warfare made horses and horse-manship highly valued, Chuang Tzu's choice of Po Lo as an emblem of the brutality of technology must have been particularly telling.

PO YI   Po Yi and Shu Ch'i were brothers. Exemplars of loyalty, after giving up a claim to their father's throne in the principality of Ku-chu, they refused to shift their feudal allegiance to Chou after it overthrew Shang, and died of starvation on the side of Mount Shouyang.

THE POWER OF VIRTUE   This is our translation of the Chinese term *te*, usually translated as power *or* as virtue. It is the power found when one identifies with Tao and is thus able to practice nondoing with perfect effect. This is virtuous behavior in a mystical, rather than conventional, sense. It is ultimate power, but like nondoing itself, it is conditioned by facts and fate. The ultimate power of a waterfall is different from the ultimate power of a human being, even when both are fully realized.

SHEN-T'U TI   An ad hoc creation, apparently. We are not sure what all the tree and pillar hugging is about in chapter 29.

SHIH   Shih Yu, a historical paragon of Confucian righteousness, is paired with Tseng Shen (Tseng Tzu) to embody the more rigid of the Confucian virtues.

SHOUYANG   Also known as Thunderhead Mountain, it is located east of the great northward bend of the Yellow River in the heart of Shang and early Chou territory.

SHUN   The second of the Three Sage Emperors, Yao chose Shun as joint ruler and successor on the basis of his filial piety. There are several wonderful mythical tales about the trials he endured as a youth.

SLAVE CREEK   There are several streams with this name in present and historical China, but it appears that the name was most likely chosen by the author for its thematic suggestiveness. (*See* Warrior River.)

SUNG   A small state in the center of Chou dynasty China, on the south side of the Yellow River in its middle reaches. The Yellow River shifted its bed disastrously several times in recorded history, reaching the sea either north or south of the Shantung peninsula. One of the prime southern alternate courses to the sea ran through the middle of Sung. Sung was also the home of the philosopher Mo Tzu. For some reason (anti–Mo Tzu propaganda?), its people often appear to have been the butt of jokes about their stupidity.

TAO   The Way. Lao Tzu says, in Ursula Le Guin's translation,

> The way you can
> go isn't the real way.
> The name you can say
> isn't the real name.*

A major identifying feature of the Way is that words falsify it. Chuang Tzu avoids the term wherever possible, for the obvious reason. The author of chapter 31 of the *Chuang Tzu*, through the persona of the foolish Confucius, speaking of the Old Fisherman, provides us with an operational definition:

> Now, the Tao is that of which all the ten thousand things are followers. All things that get it live; all things that lose it die. To turn from it in your work is to be defeated; to follow it is completion.

THE TEN THOUSAND THINGS   This term has been generally conceived of by translators as meaning all phenomena. We are inclined to believe it is limited to all living things, but we aren't altogether sure what Chuang Tzu considered to be nonliving.

T'IEN CH'ENG-TZU   A historical character. The text of *Chuang Tzu* is corrupt here with regard to the timing of his usurpation, but the man exists in other historical texts of the period.

TIGER YANG   A generic bandit. This family name is the Yang of yin and yang, indicating his fiery nature, which, taken to an extreme, makes him a Tiger. The lines he appears in are among the funniest ironic anticlimaxes in all the world's literature. The joke's on Confucius, as it usually is in the *Chuang Tzu*, outside the "Inner Chapters" at least.

TSENG TZU   Tseng Shen, or Master Tseng, was a major disciple of Confucius. An exemplar of filial piety, he is sometimes held responsible for the overemphasis on that single virtue in Confucian orthodoxies from the Han dynasty onward. He is paired with Shih Yu to embody the more rigid of the Confucian virtues.

* *Lao Tzu, Tao Te Ching: A Book About the Way and the Power of the Way* (Boston: Shambhala Publications, 1997).

TZU-CHANG Historically, a disciple of Confucius. Keep in mind that, like Confucius himself in these pages, all the disciples are subject to the humorous whims of the author.

TZU-HSU A loyal and sagacious minister who aided several kings of the southern state of Wu in their ongoing struggle against the neighboring state of Yueh.

TZU-KUNG Another disciple of Confucius, also called Tuan-mu Ssu, he was particularly known for his eloquence.

TZU-LU Disciple and military *aide de camp* to Confucius. In the *Analects*, there is a very clear bond of affection between the two very different men. The authors of the *Chuang Tzu* trade on the reader's knowledge of that bond.

TZU SANG An ad hoc creation; the name means "Mr. Mulberry."

TZU YU An ad hoc creation; the name means "Mr. Chariot."

WARRIOR RIVER Neither ancient commentaries nor modern geographical works offer any indication that this place name corresponds to an actual location. As with Slave Creek (also in chapter 17, "Autumn Floods"), the name seems chosen for its suggestive effect. It highlights the philosophical conflict between Chuang Tzu and his friend Hui Tzu, and lets Chuang Tzu cap his nonsensical linguistic trickery in the passage with a pun at the combative sophist's expense.

WEI, WEY, WAY Feudal states whose names are written with completely different characters but are transliterated the same (traditionally as Wei).

WU Semi-barbarous area in what was in Chuang Tzu's time far southeast China. In the expanded geographical area of modern China, the same area is in east central China. It was proverbially at war with the neighboring state of Yueh.

YANG CHU The thought of Yang Chu, a historical person (fourth century BCE), is regarded as foreshadowing Taoism per se. He appears to have advocated a fairly selfish egoism but was not a hedonist. His relatively self-centered philosophy makes a matched pair with Mo Tzu's self-sacrificing idealism.

YAO   The first of the Three Sage Emperors who preceded the foundation of the legendary Hsia dynasty, Yao ignored his own son, married two of his daughters to Shun, and passed the throne on to him. The basis of the Chinese attitudes toward legitimate sovereignty can be found in the myths dealing with Yao, Shun, and Yu the Great. Historicized myths about the trio of Wen, Wu, and Chou Kung, founders of the Chou dynasty, further explicate the issues. Confucius idealizes both sets. Chuang Tzu brings them back to earth.

YELLOW EMPEROR   Huang Ti, the Yellow Emperor, the mythic founder of the Chinese polity, was a culture hero credited with many inventions essential to civilized life. The two schools of Taoism after Chuang Tzu are called Huang-Lao (the school of the Yellow Emperor and Lao Tzu) and Lao-Chuang (the school of Lao Tzu and Chuang Tzu). The former school was the basis for magical popular religions, and the latter for elite philosophical thought. The attitude of the authors of the *Chuang Tzu* toward the mythical Yellow Emperor is one of unfaltering mockery, as might be expected under the circumstances. Chuang Tzu has no truck with such a mundane thing as the simply supernatural.

YEN HUI   Also called Yen Yuan, he was the favorite disciple of Confucius. Brilliant, and an exceptionally sensitive and hard-working student, he died young.

YI   Yi and P'eng meng are legendary master archers.

YU THE GREAT   Third of the Three Sage Emperors, he worked for years to drain away the "great flood" (drain and control the Yellow River delta and estuaries) and was rewarded with the throne by Shun. He passed it on to his own son, thereby beginning the Hsia dynasty, the first (protohistorical?) period of rule by ordinary humans.

YUEH   Anciently, a state identified with the southeast coast of modern China. It was proverbially at war with its neighbor, Wu.